TI-83 PLUS
&
SILVER EDITION MANUAL

for
STATISTICS

Stephen Kelly

PEARSON

Prentice
Hall

Upper Saddle River, NJ 07458

Acquisitions Editor: Petra Recter
Supplement Editor: Joanne Wendelken
Executive Managing Editor: Vince O'Brien
Production Editor: Jeffrey Rydell
Supplement Cover Manager: Paul Gourhan
Supplement Cover Designer: Joanne Alexandris
Manufacturing Buyer: Ilene Kahn

© 2005 Pearson Education, Inc.
Pearson Prentice Hall
Pearson Education, Inc.
Upper Saddle River, NJ 07458

Printed in the United States of America

10 9 8 7 6 5 4 3 2 1

ISBN 0-13-148023-5

Pearson Education Ltd., *London*
Pearson Education Australia Pty. Ltd., *Sydney*
Pearson Education Singapore, Pte. Ltd.
Pearson Education North Asia Ltd., *Hong Kong*
Pearson Education Canada, Inc., *Toronto*
Pearson Educación de Mexico, S.A. de C.V.
Pearson Education—Japan, *Tokyo*
Pearson Education Malaysia, Pte. Ltd.

Table Of Contents

Note to students

This supplement has been written with you, the student, in mind. It is intended as a guide to help you learn the functions of the TI-83PLUS graphing calculator as it applies to an introductory Statistics course. The TI-83PLUS graphing calculator can be used for many other purposes, and this book may not be sufficient explanation for courses other than an introductory Statistics course. I have tried to show all screens that will be encountered while performing a particular calculation on the TI.

This supplement is not intended to teach the concepts of Statistics. Its purpose is to help you with the graphing calculator. For this reason it is assumed that you, the student, have a basic understanding of the statistical process you want to perform. This book will use many statistical terms without giving a thorough explanation of the term itself. Please do not expect this handbook to explain Elementary Statistics.

The sections presented within this handbook are not completely independent. For best results the student should start at page 1 and work through each example in sequence towards the end of the book.

At the end of this handbook there is a copy of some programs that might be helpful in a general statistics course along with a brief description of each. I have included a few pages on ERROR messages.

I have arranged the sections in this book to follow the order of presentation in an Elementary Statistics course. I hope the mini-lessons within this handbook will be self-explanatory and help ease the anxiety associated with using the graphing calculator.

I believe that the graphing calculator allows us to spend more time concentrating on the concepts of Statistics and less time with the arithmetic.

It is for this reason that I feel all students should be knowledgeable on the graphing calculator, as well as several available statistics software. Even though I have tried to foresee every problem, there will undoubtedly be those times that you will be "stuck." I have included my e-mail address for that reason.

You may e-mail me: skelly1@uwf.edu

Getting Started With the TI-83Plus & Silver

Important Note: If you purchased a **used** calculator your first step is to return the calculator to its original default settings. Follow these steps: Turn `ON` the calculator. Then to reset to original settings as follows:
For the **TI-83 Plus & Silver Addition:**
Press: `2nd` `+` `4` `ENTER`   This will clear all Lists
Press: `2nd` `+` `7` `2` `2` `ENTER`   This will reset the calculator

This will help you avoid most unwanted **"ERROR"** messages.

NOTE: I have added a section on error messages. While it is impossible to address every error that may be encountered by a graphing calculator user, I have devoted a few pages to the most common types of errors my students seem to encounter.

After you finish each problem *Press:* `CLEAR` to return to the home screen. **It may take more than one time**.
It is a good idea to begin each new problem from the home screen.☺

One feature of the TI-83 Plus & Silver Addition is the use of Scientific Notation when displayed values are of extreme quantities.
(*i.e. 2.33454332E-7 is the calculator's notation for the value 0.000000233454332*) When reading a displayed value take care to read across the entire line. The calculator will always use Scientific Notation for extreme values whether it is set in Scientific MODE or not. Be sure you are familiar with Scientific Notation.

Lastly, the calculator can convert fractions to decimals and decimals to fractions. (*Some decimal approximations represent irrational numbers and of course they cannot be converted into fractions*)

For example: if you have the fraction **7/11** on your screen and you want to convert it to a decimal
press : `MATH` ▼ `ENTER` `ENTER`   **.6363636364** will be displayed.
(This is the decimal approximation for 7/11)

To convert it back to a fraction *press*: `MATH` `ENTER` `ENTER`
7/11 will be displayed.

Entering Data and Plotting Graphs

Use this sample list : **3, 4, 4, 5, 5, 6, 6, 7, 8**
To enter data into the calculator, 1ˢᵗ *press* `STAT` (this screen will appear)

"**EDIT**" will be highlighted. Then *press* `ENTER`
This brings you to the screen showing these list: (*always start from a clear List*)

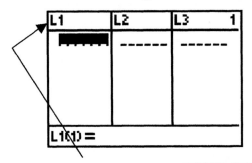

*To clear **List 1** highlight "L1" and press* `CLEAR` `ENTER`

Enter each piece of data making sure to press **ENTER** after each entry.

To calculate the basic statistics after you have entered the data into **list 1**
you first *press* `STAT` (you will see screen below)

Then **Arrow right** to **"CALC".** " **1:1-Var Stats"** must be highlighted .
Press `ENTER` (see screen on p.2)

Now to see a display of basic descriptive statistics from **List 1** you must *press* **2nd** **1** **ENTER** (For **List 2** you would press 2nd **2**, etc.)(see screen below)

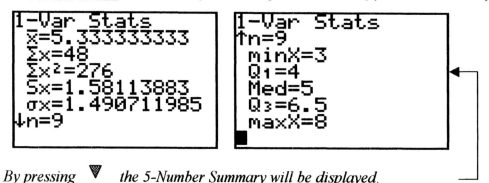

By pressing ▼ *the 5-Number Summary will be displayed.*

For most graphs in this course you may press **ZOOM** **9** *to have the calculator automatically adjust the window to the data. You must know which LIST(S) you want to graph. The calculator will graph from any LIST.*

To graph a **histogram** of the data entered into **list 1** you *press* **2nd** **Y =**
    " **1: Plot1…**" should appear highlighted, (see below left)

Press **ENTER** (see above right) Now " **ON** " must be highlighted then

Press **ENTER** (the screen will not appear different)

Next, Arrow down and right to _____ *press* **ENTER**

Make sure **Xlist: L1** , **Freq: 1** *Press* WINDOW to adjust your settings to match those on page 3. *[L1, L2, L3, etc. are found as 2nd functions above 1, 2, 3 etc.]*

The Xscl is the "class width." *You **must** adjust it to fit your problem.*

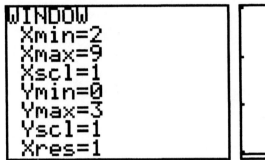 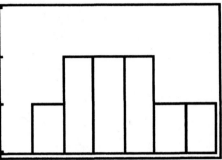

Now *press* GRAPH (the top right histogram will appear.)
As with any graph, *press* TRACE to display all important values.
        Simply **Arrow right** or **Arrow left** to see the desired values.

It is important to learn how to adjust the window settings to fit each problem; however, one feature of the TI-83PLUS is **ZOOMStat**. By using **ZOOMStat** the **calculator** will choose a window to fit the data. Lets see this same histogram using **ZOOMStat**. Simply *press* ZOOM Arrow down to **"9: ZOOMStat"** *press* ENTER (you will see this screen)

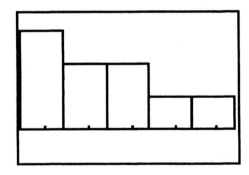

You can see from this screen **ZOOMStat** does **not** necessarily give the **best** view.

To use **ZOOMStat** omit all steps following **"make sure XLIST: L1, Freq. : 1** **"** *Press* ZOOM Arrow down to **"9: ZOOMStat"** and *press* ENTER

[You may graph up to 3 plots on the same screen, provided they have similar domain. Use plot#1 for graph1, plot#2 for graph2, plot#3 for graph3.]

Graphing a BoxPlot

Drawing a boxplot on the TI-83Plus is the same procedure as drawing a histogram except for 1 step. Consider the example problem above.
Let's use the same sample list : **3, 4, 4, 5, 5, 6, 6, 7, 8**
To enter the data turn on the calculator and *press*: STAT ENTER you will see these two screens as you press each of the buttons:

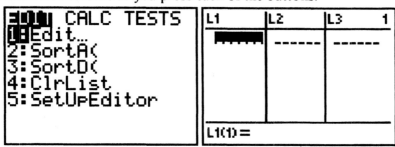

This is the LISTS Menu. You will be using this screen every time you enter data into the calculator. (The only exception is when entering data for a χ2 test. You will then use the matrix menu)
Type each number followed then *press:* ENTER

Once you have entered all the data *press*: Y=

You will see this screen.

This is the Statistical Plots Menu.
Whenever you want to plot a graph you will need to adjust the parameters within this menu. You may graph up to 3 things on the same screen by turning on up to 3 Plots.

For now we only want 1 plot (a Boxplot) of the data we just entered so we will only turn "on" Plot1. To enter the parameters section *press*: ENTER
After pressing the enter key you will enter the highlighted plot.

Press: ENTER *This will turn the Plot on. You will notice the highlighted switch was moved to "On" as you pressed enter.*

For our current problem we will highlight Boxplot with outliers,
by following these steps.

Press: ▼   ▶   ▶   ▶   This will highlight the Boxplot.
Press: ENTER
Press: ▼   Beside the *"Xlist :"* you must enter the list where
Press: 2nd 1   you put your data. (I used List1)

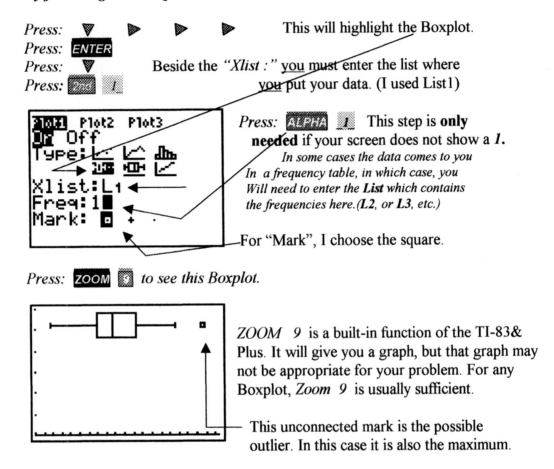

Press: ALPHA 1   This step is **only**
needed if your screen does not show a *1*.
In some cases the data comes to you
In a frequency table, in which case, you
*Will need to enter the **List** which contains*
*the frequencies here.(**L2**, or **L3**, etc.)*

—For "Mark", I choose the square.

Press: ZOOM 9 *to see this Boxplot.*

ZOOM 9 is a built-in function of the TI-83 &
Plus. It will give you a graph, but that graph may
not be appropriate for your problem. For any
Boxplot, *Zoom 9* is usually sufficient.

This unconnected mark is the possible
outlier. In this case it is also the maximum.

Press: TRACE and the calculator will display several characteristics of the graph.
For a Boxplot it will display the minimum, Q1, Median, Q3, lower fence(s),
Maximum, one number at a time by flashing the curser on the appropriate location
as you arrow from left to right.

Note: the calculator does not display titles, units or numerical scale. If you are
printing any graph you must add those items yourself using your favorite word
processor. The calculator is a wonderful machine but it does not "know" what
is appropriate for your problem. ☺

Frequency Tables, Plots, Printouts

To enter data from a frequency table. First enter all the data into the
calculator. Use this sample frequency distribution.

Xi	frequency
2	3
3	5
4	4
5	6
6	4
7	2

First *press* STAT , (This screen will appear)

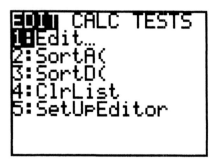

Make sure " **EDIT** " is highlighted then *press* ENTER.
(This screen will appear)

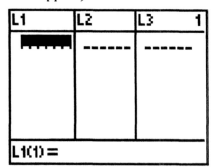

First, type all the values into **L1** , one at a time remembering to *press* ENTER
after each one.

Next, Arrow right to list 2. (*The flasher will automatically return to the top
of the list.*) Type the frequencies into **L2** remembering to press ENTER
after each one. (you will end with this next screen)

To calculate the basic descriptive statistics of this data first *press:* STAT
(the same screen will appear as on p4)

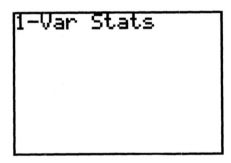

Arrow right to **"CALC"**
"1: 1-VAR STAT" should be
highlighted (Your screen will look like
this)

Now *press* ENTER

(You should see this screen)

```
1-Var Stats
```

*You must now tell the
calculator where you put the
X's and the frequencies.*

We entered the X's into **L1**
and the frequencies into **L2**

So to display the descriptive statistics *press*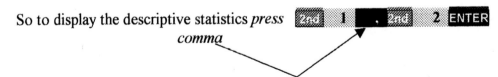
                                comma

NOTE: The list *preceding* the comma must be the list containing
the *x-values*, and the list *following* the comma must be the list
containing the corresponding *frequencies*.

This display is called the "Basic Descriptive Statistics"

```
1-Var Stats
 x̄=4.375
 Σx=105
 Σx²=513
 Sx=1.526932133
 σx=1.494782593
↓n=24
```

By pressing the Arrow down key repeatedly you may view the 5-number summary.

To see a **histogram, box plot,** or **scatter plot** from a frequency distribution you must go to the **STAT PLOT** function of the calculator. *Press* `2nd` `Y =` (This screen will appear)

" **1: Plot 1 ...**" should be highlighted, now *press* `ENTER`

(This screen will appear) Highlight **"ON"** and *press* `ENTER`

Arrow down and **right** to the desired graph. (Say a **scatter plot**)

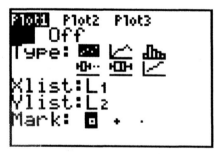

Press ENTER (see screen)

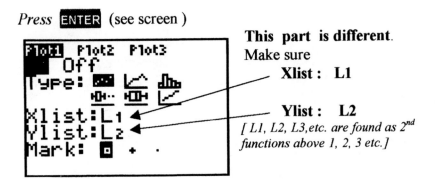

This part is different.
Make sure

    Xlist : L1

    Ylist : L2

[L1, L2, L3,etc. are found as 2ⁿᵈ
functions above 1, 2, 3 etc.]

Remember you still must adjust the WINDOW ***to fit your data, or use*** ZOOM ▯

X-min: 1 , X-max: 8 , X-scl: 1, Y-min: 0 , Y-max: 7 , X-scl: 1

Press GRAPH (this graph will appear)

*(*Again, pressing TRACE and **Arrow right** or **left** will show each value*)*

A histogram of that same data looks as follows:

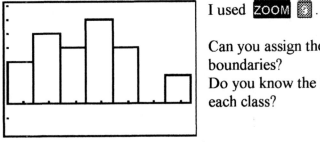

I used ZOOM ▯ .

Can you assign the class
boundaries?
Do you know the frequencies for
each class?

Example 2

We begin this problem the same as before: entering the X's into List1 and the corresponding frequencies into List2. First calculate the class marks from the table below. These will be our X's. Now enter the class marks into List1 and the corresponding frequencies into List2.

Press: STAT ENTER

As you can see my old data is still in the lists.

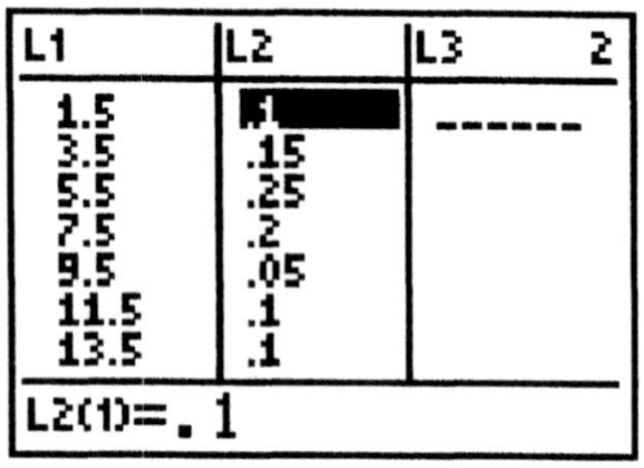

L1	L2	L3	2
1.5	.1	------	
3.5	.15		
5.5	.25		
7.5	.2		
9.5	.05		
11.5	.1		
13.5	.1		

L2(1)=.1

Recall: to clear an entire list we highlight the very top: (ie L1, L2) and Press: CLEAR ENTER

Class Marks (L1)	Magnitude	Number of Earthquakes (L2)
0.0	0	1774
0.5	0.1 – 0.9	6
1.5	1.0 – 1.9	580
2.5	2.0 – 2.9	3080
3.5	3.0 – 3.9	4518
4.5	4.0 – 4.9	5548
5.5	5.0 – 5.9	674
6.5	6.0 – 6.9	97
7.5	7.0 – 7.9	9
8.5	8.0 – 8.9	1

Once again we must adjust the window to fit our current data.
Press: WINDOW   *You will see the following screen:*

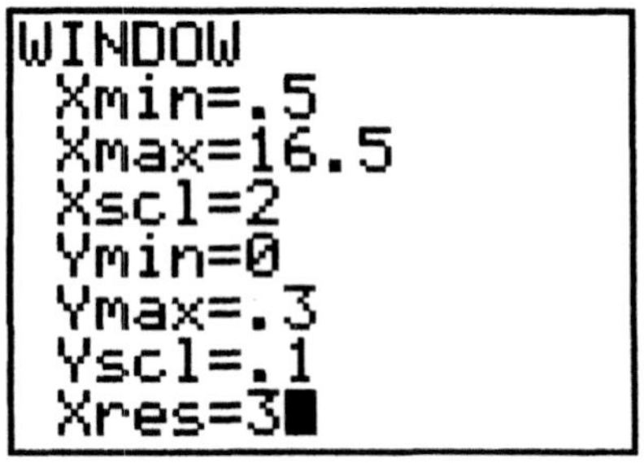

```
WINDOW
 Xmin=.5
 Xmax=16.5
 Xscl=2
 Ymin=0
 Ymax=.3
 Yscl=.1
 Xres=3
```

Recall: these are the settings from the last problem. The new settings must match our new problem.

The screen below shows the menu <u>after</u> all adjustments have been made.

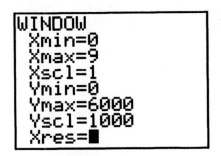

These are the settings after **you** *have made the changes.*

Since the last problem used **List1** for class marks and **List2** for frequency and we graphed a **Histogram** there are no changes needed within the **STAT PLOT** Menu.

So Press GRAPH

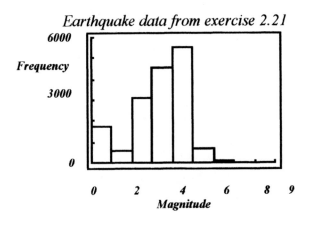

Earthquake data from exercise 2.21

Recall: *you must add the title, scales, and any necessary units needed for your problem.*

Example 3

Calculate the Basic Descriptive Statistics. Include the 5-number summary and the mode for the following data.

18, 10, 15, 13, 17, 15, 12, 15, 18, 16, 11

First enter the data into the calculator. I will use list 1.

Press: STAT ENTER

This will take you to the Lists Menu.

Clear any old data from the list as it may interfere with this new problem.

After you have entered all the data *Press:* STAT ▷ ENTER

```
1-Var Stats ∎
```

At this time you must enter the list designation where you placed the data. Since I put the data in List 1, I will *press:* 2nd 1.

Next *Press:* ENTER

The TI-83 will display many different statistics. Some you will need, some you will not need. I will point out the basic statistics most often asked for.

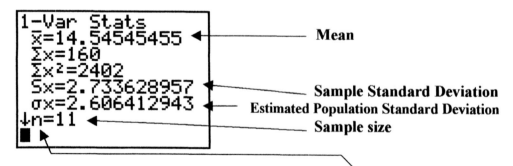

Notice the arrow pointing downward in front of the n=11. This tells us there is more data that can be seen by pressing the arrow down key.

Press: ▼ a few times and you will see this new screen.

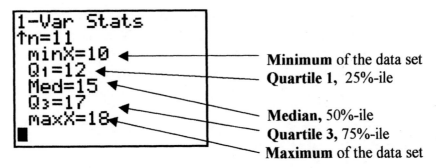

```
1-Var Stats
↑n=11
  minX=10  ◄──────────────  Minimum of the data set
  Q₁=12    ◄──────────────  Quartile 1, 25%-ile
  Med=15   ◄
  Q₃=17
  maxX=18◄
  ■
```

Minimum of the data set
Quartile 1, 25%-ile

Median, 50%-ile
Quartile 3, 75%-ile
Maximum of the data set

Together these two screens give you most everything wanted when someone asks for "the basic descriptive statistics."

The mode is, of course, the piece of data with the highest frequency.

For this problem the **mode** = __15__ as it appears the most: three times.

COMPUTER PRINTOUTS

You can capture any screen that appears on your calculator with the help of " **TI-GRAPHLINK**. " or **"TI CONNECT"** You may also use these software to send or receive Lists, or Programs between the PC and Calculator. You may also use this program to download freeware from the TI Website, or data from a variety of Statistical data sources.

   To obtain a printout from your calculator you must have the screen you want a picture of appearing on your calculator. You can only print 1 screen at a time, and it must be showing on your calculator . Lets say you want to print the screen showing the descriptive statistics from the frequency distribution above. Make sure it is showing on your calculator screen. Go to a computer that has the **GRAPHLINK** cable attached to the computer and follow these steps:.

1. Plug the cable into the bottom of your calculator ..
2. Using the mouse double click on the Icon " **TI-83PLUS GRAPHLINK"** .   [Wait a few seconds]
3. Using the mouse click on the word   **"LINK "** . This will pull down a menu of options.
4. Using the mouse Click on " **Get Screen**". Choose **"Get Screen".**
   [*You can send the screen capture to the computer clipboard. Once you open a WORD document the capture can be pasted onto the document by pressing* **"CTRL   V "** *on the computer keyboard.*
5. The menu will change again and using the mouse you should click on **"PRINT "**
6. A printout of the screen will be sent to the printer.

Remember the printout will only show exactly what the screen shows. It **does not** print the necessary units associated with your problem!! **You must** add them **yourself !** (e.g. graph titles, $, lb., cm, m, days, etc. **must** be added by you, the student)

   "TI-Graphlink" and **"TI CONNECT"** are freeware available from the TI website. The cable can be purchased separately or with the software.

The Counting Principle & Probability

When choosing between *permutations* or *combinations* you must first decide whether or not **order** is important.

If it **is** important then you are performing a permutation.

If it **is not** important then you are performing a combination .

To calculate a permutation on the calculator start from a clear screen .

To calculate say **5 !** First *press* 5 , next press MATH (see lower left)

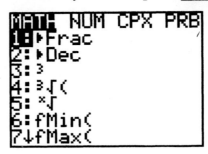   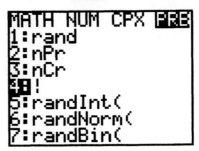

Now **Arrow left** to " **PRB** " Highlight " **4 : !** " . (see upper right screen)

    Press ENTER   (your screen will now look like this)

Press ENTER.   **120**   will be displayed on the right of the screen.

This is of course the number of permutations of **5** objects, or stated differently: it is the number of ways you can arrange **5** objects.

Suppose you only want to arrange some of the objects from a group.

There is a different operation on the calculator for just such a desire.

To calculate the permutation of **3** objects from a set of **7** objects , **(7P3)**
Start from a clear screen.   First press **7** , then press **MATH**
Arrow left to **"PRB"** (you will see lower left screen)

 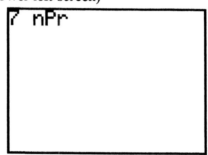

Highlight **" 2 : nPr"** *Press* **ENTER** (upper right screen will appear)
Now press **3** (Your screen should look like this)

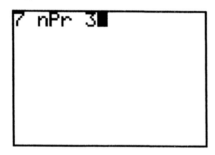

Press **ENTER**   **210** will be displayed . This is the number of permutations
of **3** objects from a group of **7** objects. Said another way : it is the number of
ways you can **arrange** any **3** objects from a list of **7** objects.
So far the order of the objects **is** important because we have been calculating
permutations.

If order is **not** important then you want to perform a combination.

In a combination we are simply interested in the number of ways that objects
can be selected.

If order **does matter** >>>>>>>>>>> **permutation.**

If order **does not matter** >>>>>>>>>>>**combination.**

Next we will work a combination problem

Example 2

Say we want to choose **3** objects from a list of **7** objects, **(7C3)** .

Start from a clear screen.

First press ⬛ 7 ⬛ , next press MATH (this screen will appear)

Arrow left to " **PRB** " and highlight " **3 : nCr** " .

Press ENTER (this screen will be displayed)

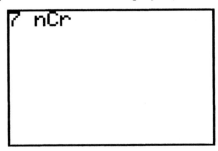

Press ⬛ 3 ⬛ ENTER , (this screen will appear) .

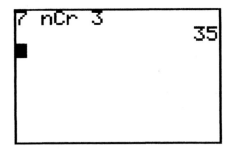

35 is the number of combinations of **3** objects from **7** objects.

Stated another way ; it is the number of ways you can choose **3** objects from a list of **7** objects .

Example 3

Permute 5 objects from a group of 5 objects. We could actually use " ! "
as before, but for this problem lets use the new Permutations rule from the **Math**
Menu on the calculator.

On the calculator it will look slightly different. It will look as follows:
(nPr), *where the n ~ total number of items, and r ~ the number being permuted.*

Start from a clear screen. First *press:* 5 then *press:* MATH
Press: ◀ to highlight " **PRB** "

```
MATH NUM CPX PRB
1:rand
2:nPr
3:nCr
4:!
5:randInt(
6:randNorm(
7:randBin(
```

```
5 nPr ■
```

Arrow down and Highlight " **2 : nPr** " *Press:* ENTER (see screen above)

Press: 5

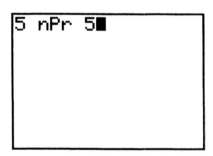

```
5 nPr 5■
```

(Your screen should now look like this)

Press: ENTER
120 *will be displayed . This is the number of permutations of 5 objects*
from a group of 5 objects.

So **5P5** = 120. Which is exactly the same thing as **5!**

Example 4

Find the number of ways you can choose 5 objects from a group of 100 objects. This is a <u>combination</u> problem. We are interested in the number of ways that objects can be selected.

For this problem we will also use different notation on the calculator as follows: **nCr** *where the n ~ total number of items, and r ~ the number being chosen.* Start from a clear screen.

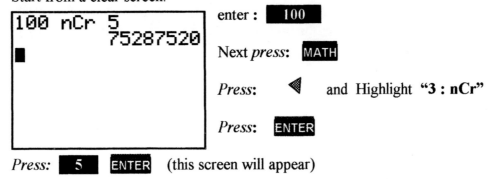

enter : **100**

Next *press*: MATH

Press: ◀   and Highlight **"3 : nCr"**

Press: ENTER

Press: **5** ENTER   (this screen will appear)

75,287,520 is the number of combinations of 5 objects from 100 objects.

Stated another way; it is the number of ways you can choose 5 objects from a list of 100 objects.

Remember permutations and combinations are two different counting procedures.

You must decide if the order of the objects is important!

*If it <u>**does matter**</u> what order they are in >>>>>>>>>>> **permutation.**
*If it <u>**does not matter**</u> what order the objects are in >>>>><u>**combination.**</u>

Discrete Probability Functions

The **Binomial Probability Function** can be used to calculate the probability of **"x"** successes from **"n"** trials with the probability of success on each trial **"p"**. We say **"x"**, the random variable, is distributed Binomial**(n,p,x).**

Example 1

Say we want to calculate the probability of **3** successes from a total of **10** independent trials where the probability of success on each trial is **0.35**. Here : **"n" = 10 ,"x" = 3** , and **"p"= 0.35** .

On the calculator start from a clear screen. *Press* **2nd** **VARS** (you will see this screen)

Arrow down to choice **"0: binompdf ("** *Press* **ENTER**. (you will see this screen)

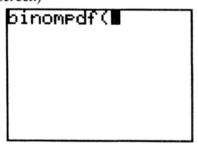

You must enter **n , p , x** in **that order** inside the parenthesis. So for our problem we will enter **10** **,** **0.35** **,** **3** **)** . *Don't forget the commas or the closed parenthesis!*
 Now *press* **ENTER** **.252219625** will be displayed.
This is the probability of **3** successes from **10** trials where the probability of success on each trial is **0.35** .
What if you wanted to know the probability of **5** successes from this same distribution?

You do not have to start over from the beginning.

To calculate the probability of **5** successes from the same problem you do not have to start over. Simply *press* 2nd ENTER (this screen will reappear)

```
binompdf(10,.35,
3)
          .252219625
binompdf(10,.35,
3)
```

Now you can **Arrow left** to highlight the   3   . Next *press*   5   This will replace the **3** with a **5**. *Press* ENTER **.1535704107** will be displayed. This is the probability of 5 successes from 10 trials where the probability of success on each trial is 0.35.

"Binomcdf (" will calculate the cumulative probability from 0 through X.

e.g. **Binomcdf (10 , .20 , 4)** will calculate the probability of **x = 0+1+2+3+4 success**, where n=10, p=0.20, which = **.9672065025**] see Example 2

Plot a Binomial Distribution

Let's use this last problem's data where **"n"= 10**, **"p"= 0.35**. First *press* STAT **"EDIT"** should be highlighted. *Press* ENTER
Make sure all list are clear. [*To clear L1 you* **Arrow up** *to and highlight* **L1**, *press* CLEAR ENTER. *Follow the same procedure to clear any list.*]

Enter the numbers **{1,2,3,4,5,6,7,8,9,10}** into **List 1.**
These are the **"x"** values. Next we want to enter a **formula** into **List 2**.
First highlight **L2** (you should see this screen)

```
L1      L2      L3      2
1       ------  ------
2
3
4
5
6
7
L2 =
```

Now press `(` `10` `MATH` Next **Arrow left** to " **PRB** "
highlight **"3: nCr"**

  Press `ENTER` `2nd` `1` `)`   (this screen will appear)

L1	L2	L3	2
1	------	------	
2			
3			
4			
5			
6			
7			

L2 =(10 nCr L1)

Next press `(` `.35` `^` `2nd` `1` `)`
You will see this text scroll across the bottom of the screen:

L1	L2	L3	2
1	------	------	
2			
3			
4			
5			
6			
7			

L2 =…L1)(.35^L1)

Now enter `(` `.65` `^` `(` `10` `-` `2nd` `1` `)` `)` .
 You will be able to see all the text by **Arrowing left** or **right** .
Now *press* `ENTER` These probabilities will appear in **List2.**   (See below)

L1	L2	L3	2
1	.07249	------	
2	.17565		
3	.25222		
4	.23767		
5	.15357		
6	.06891		
7	.0212		

L2(1)=.0724916949…

[*The numbers in **List2** are the probabilities associated with the "x" values
from **List1**.*] (i.e. The probability that **x = 5** is **0.15357, etc.)**

Now to see a plot we must go to the **STAT PLOT** so *press* 2nd Y =
(You will see this screen)

"1:Plot1..." should be highlighted. *Press* ENTER Make sure **On** is highlighted
and *press* ENTER (You should be looking at this screen)

Arrow down and highlight the first option right of **"Type"** (Scatter Plot)
And *press* ENTER Make sure **Xlist: L1** , **Ylist: L2**

Now, as always, we need to adjust the **window** to fit our data or you may
press ZOOM ▢ *to have the calculator automatically adjust the window.*

Press WINDOW **Xmin: 0** , **Xmax: 11** , **Xscl 1** , **Ymin: 0** ,
Ymax: 0.5 , **Yscl 0.1**

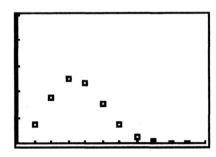

Press GRAPH (this screen will appear)
Notice that even with only 10 data points this graph resembles a "bell curve."

You can read the probabilities directly off this screen. *Press* `TRACE`

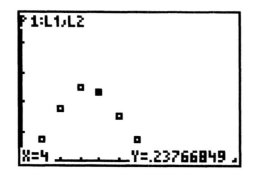

Arrow right or **Left**

Here "**x**" is the number of successes and "**y**" is the corresponding probability.
So from this screen we see that there is a .**2377** chance of **4** successes from
10 trials where the probability of success on each trial is **0.35**.

[You can **Arrow left** or **right** to read each desired probability.]
*Notice also that in the upper left screen P1: L1,L2 is displayed. This tells us
that we are using PLOT1 and the data from LIST1, and LIST2.*

Example 2
Find the following probabilities using **p = .80,** and **n = 10**
a) **P(x = 3)**   b) **P(x < 7)**   c) **P(x > 4)**
We will need to work 3 different problems: 1 for part a, 1 for part b, 1 for part c.
a.   **P(x = 3)**   *Press:* `2nd` `VARS`
(you will see this screen)

 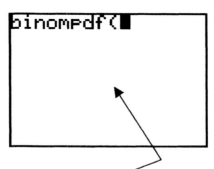

Arrow down to "**0: binompdf (**"
 Press: `ENTER`   (you will see this screen)
You must enter **n , p , x** *in that order inside the parenthesis.*
For our problem

*Press:*_ 10 , 0 .80 , 3)_

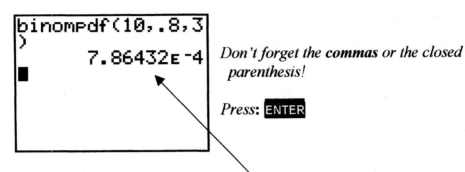

Don't forget the **commas** *or the closed parenthesis!*

Press: ENTER

Note: The answer is given in **Scientific Notation.**
In common notation it = **0.000786432**

b. P(x < 7)   For this part   *Press:* 2nd VARS

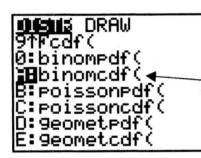

This is not the same as part a.
!!! Look carefully !!!

Arrow down to "**A: binomcdf ("**
Press: ENTER

On the TI-83 the ending "cdf" will calculate a cumulative frequency, starting
from 0 and continuing up to and including the number you enter.
Everything else will work the same. Enter **n** , **p** , **x** in that order.
For our problem we enter **10 , .80 , 7)** *See left screen*

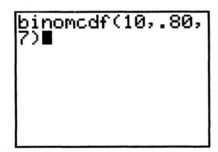
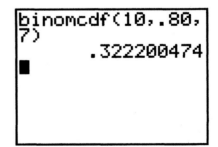

Press: ENTER
As can be seen from the right screen P(x < 7) = **.322200474**

c. P(x > 4)   Recall: this is the complement to P(x < 4) which can be done
                 directly on the calculator.

We will work the complementary event and subtract that answer from 1
giving P(x > 4).   Remember **1 – P(E') = P(E)**

Press: 2nd ENTER

```
binomcdf(10,.80,
7)
        .322200474
binomcdf(10,.80,
7)▮
```

You will see this screen.

Next, **Arrow left** *and replace the* 7 *with a* **4**

Press: ENTER

```
binomcdf(10,.80,
7)
        .322200474
binomcdf(10,.80,
4)
      .0063693824
▮
```

*We now need to subtract this complementary
event from 1 to get our answer:*

1 - .0063693824 = .9936306176

So P(x > 4) = **.9936306176**

POISSON Probability Function

The **POISSON Probability Function** is a discrete probability distribution function used to calculate the number of successes "**x**" from some **given interval** where the probability of success on each **standard interval** is the same. We say "**x**", the random variable, is distributed POISSON **(λ,x).**

[*To calculate the probability of random variables which are distributed POISSON we will follow a very similar procedure to the one just described.*]

Example 1

Let's say we want to find the probability of **4** flaws in a **10** yard piece of material where it is known that this material has an average of only **1** flaw every **5** yards. Here our *given* interval is __10__ yards. Our *standard* interval **is __5__** yards, and "**x**" is __4__.

We first need to calculate our expected value, λ, for **10** yards. We will use the information given:

(1flaw / 5yards) * **10** yards = **2** flaws. This is our **μ** .We would use the formula: **P(x) = [(λ^x)(e^(-(λ)] / x !** with λ=2 and x=4.

On the calculator we go to the distribution menu and *Press* 2nd VARS Next **Arrow up** to "**B : poissonpdf (**". (this screen will be displayed)

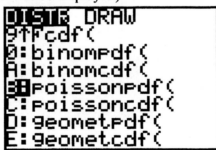

Press ENTER (you will see the screen below)

Now we must enter λ , x in that order so for our problem we enter
2 ▮ **. 4** ▮ **)** . *Press* ▮ENTER▮ **.0902235222** will be displayed.
This is the probability of **4** flaws in **10** yards of material where it is known
that the material has on the average only **1** flaw every **5** yards.

"Poissoncdf (" will give the cumulative probability from 0 through X.
(e.g. **poissoncdf (2,4)** will give the probability of **x = 0+1+2+3+4** , where λ=2**)**
You should get 0.9473469827 for the cumulative answer.

To see a **Distribution Plot** of a particular **POISSON** distribution we will
need to enter some data into the **LIST**.

We will enter the "**x**" values {**1,2,3,4,5,6,7,8,9,10**} into **L1** and the
POISSON Formula into **L2** .
Press ▮STAT▮   **"EDIT"** should be highlighted.
Press ▮ENTER▮   Make sure all list are clear.
Enter the numbers {**1,2,3,4,5,6,7,8,9,10**} into **List1**. These are the "**x**" values.
Next we want to enter the **formula** into **List2**.
First highlight **L2**   (you should see lower left screen)

L1	L2	L3	2
1			
2	------	------	
3			
4			
5			
6			
7			
L2 =			

L1	L2	L3	2
1			
2	------	------	
3			
4			
5			
6			
7			
L2 =...1)(e^(-L1)) ▮			

Next enter **(2** ^ **2nd 1) (2nd LN (-) 2nd 1))** .
(You should see this text scroll across the screen)
We now need to finish the formula by dividing by **L1** factorial .
So *press* **÷ 2nd 1** MATH (see lower left screen)

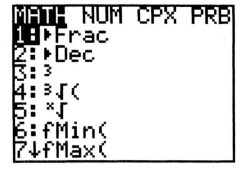
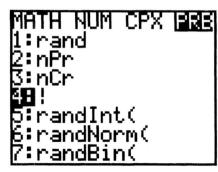

Arrow left to "**PRB**" and *press* **4** (see upper screen)

Now *press* ENTER **List2** will be filled with these probabilities
(see screen below)

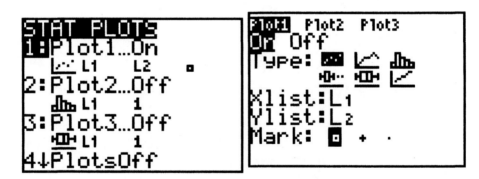

The numbers in **List2** are the probabilities associated with the **"x"** values in **List1**.

To see a plot we must go to the **STAT PLOT** so *press* 2nd Y=

"**1:Plot1...**" should be highlighted. *Press:* ENTER (see upper right screen)

Make sure **On** is highlighted and *press* ENTER

Next **Arrow down** and highlight the **plot** option. *Press* ENTER

Make sure **Xlist: L1 , Ylist: L2**

Now, as always, we need to adjust the **window** to fit our data, or you may *press* ZOOM ▓ To adjust the window *press* WINDOW
Match these settings:

Xmin: 0 , Xmax: 11 ,Xscl 1 , Ymin: 0 ,Ymax: 0.8 , Yscl 0.1 .

Press GRAPH then *press* TRACE (you will see this screen)

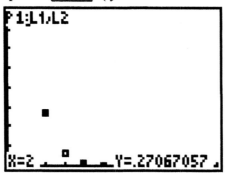

(Notice this graph more closely resembles a negative exponential curve rather than a "bell curve" like we saw from the Binomial plot)

Here "**x**" is the number of successes and "**y**" is the corresponding probability.

So from this screen we see that there is a **.27067057** probability of **2** flaws from **10** yards of material where there is an average of only **1** flaw every **5** yards. You can **Arrow left** or **right** to read each desired probability.

Notice also that in the upper left screen P1: L1,L2 is displayed. This tells us that we are using PLOT1 and the data from LIST1, and LIST2.

Example 2

Assume that x has approximately a Poisson probability distribution and that the average number for an event is 2.6 events per week.

   a) Find the probability that fewer than 2 events occur in 1 week.
   b) Find the probability that more than 5 events occur in 1 week.
   c) Find the probability that exactly 5 events occur in 1 week.

   So μ = 2.6, and x < 2 for a, x > 5 for b, and x = 5 for c

a) We want to find the probability of "fewer than 2" which means
P(x < 2) and we have given information λ = **2.6**

On the calculator we go to the distribution menu.

Press: 2nd VARS

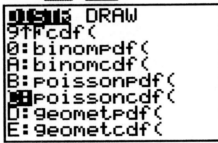

Arrow down to "C : poissoncdf ("

Press: ENTER
(you will see the screen below)

poissoncdf(▪

Now we must enter λ *,* x *)* *in that order.*

For our problem we enter **2.6** , **1**)

Press: ENTER

P(x < 2) means x = 0, or x = 1
So we must enter x = 1

As can be seen from the screen
P(x < 2) is **0.2673848816**

32

b. Here we are looking for P(x > 5). λ still equals 2.6.
We will use the complement of the event to find our answer.
The complement to P(x > 5) is P(x ≤ 5).

After we calculate the probability for the complementary event we will
subtract that answer from 1 giving P(x > 5).

Poissoncdf(2.6,5) = .9509628481
So..... P(x > 5) = 1 - .9509628481 = **.0490371519**

c. For this part we are looking for P(x = 5) so this will be
"B:Poisson**pdf**" Again λ = 2.6.

On the calculator we go to the distribution menu

Press: **2nd** **VARS**

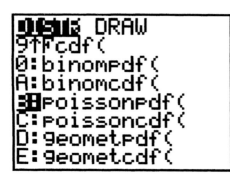

Arrow down to "B : poissonpdf ("

Press: **ENTER**

You need only enter λ , x) For our problem we
Press: **2.6** , **5** **)** **ENTER**

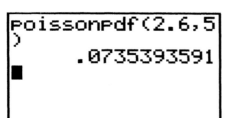

As can be seen from the screen
P(x = 5) is **.0735393591**

Standard Normal Distribution

When calculating the probability of an event using the Normal Distribution Function there are two main categories from which you may choose on the calculator:

1. **Standard Normal (using Z-scores)**
2. **Normal (using the raw data)**

Example 1   **Standard Normal Distribution**

Lets say we want to find the area under the curve between **z = -1** and **z = 1.**
This is the probability that an event is "within 1 standard deviation of the mean."
We know from the Empirical Rule that this probability should be about 68%.

On the calculator we need to go to the distributions menu.
First *press* **2nd** **VARS** (see below left)

Highlight **"2 : normalcdf("**   and *press* **ENTER** (below right)

We need to enter only two values into the parenthesis.
They must be in this order: **lower limit   ,   upper limit)**

So for our problem we will enter **(-)**   **1**   **,**   **1**   **)**   **ENTER**
Remember the negative symbol is the gray button not the blue button.

.6826894809 will be displayed. This is the probability that an event will fall within **1** standard deviation of the mean value. Or stated another way it is the area under the Standard Normal curve between **–1** and **1**.

To see a **graph** of this same problem we first need to adjust the WINDOW.
So *press* WINDOW (this screen will appear)

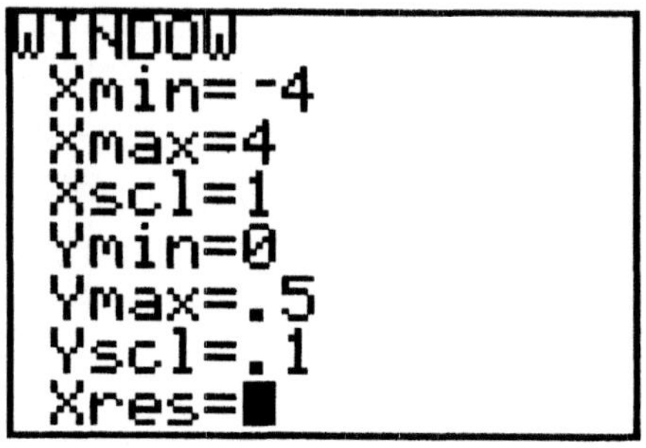

```
WINDOW
 Xmin= -4
 Xmax=4
 Xscl=1
 Ymin=0
 Ymax=.5
 Yscl=.1
 Xres=■
```

Make sure **your** settings match the above screen.
Next return to the distributions menu. Go back to this screen:

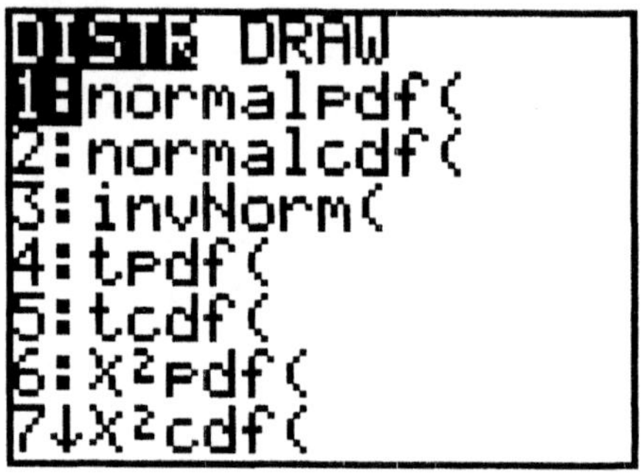

```
DISTR DRAW
1:normalpdf(
2:normalcdf(
3:invNorm(
4:tpdf(
5:tcdf(
6:X²pdf(
7↓X²cdf(
```

From this screen **Arrow right** and highlight "**DRAW** " .   Notice that
"**1 : ShadeNorm(** " is Highlighted.   *Press* ENTER (see screen below)

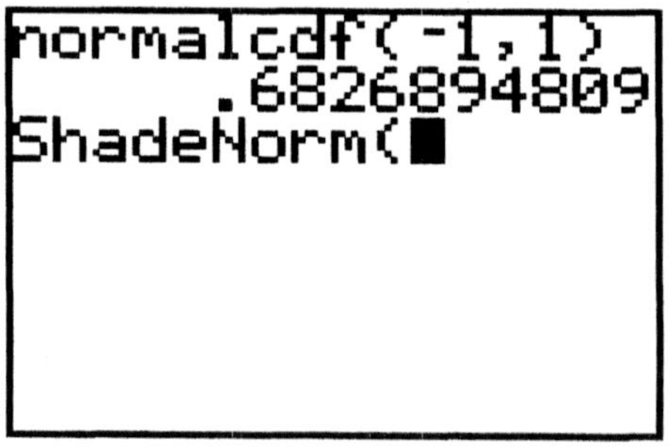

```
normalcdf(-1,1)
       .6826894809
ShadeNorm(■
```

We need to enter the same two pieces of data in the same order.
So we will enter ((-)   1   ,   1   )

Now *press* ENTER

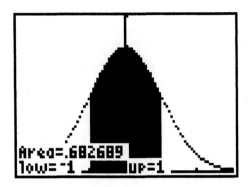

Notice that this graph displays the area as well as the lower, and upper limits.

[You can find the area under the curve between any two Z-scores using either one of these methods just described.]

If your Z-scores fall below −4 , or above 4 then you will need to adjust the X-Min, and X-Max in the WINDOW menu to fit your Z-scores.

To clear this screen *press* **2nd** **PRGM** "**clrdraw**" will be highlighted.
Press **ENTER** *Always start each new problem from the home screen*

Example 2   Standard Normal Distribution

Find the probability that a standard normal random variable lies to the left of 0.67.
Here we are trying to find the area under the curve so we use "**2:normalcdf**"
Press: **2nd** **VARS**

Highlight option "**2:normalcdf (**"

Press **ENTER**

*Recall for **Standard** Normal Distribution we need only enter 2 values: **lower** , **upper***

For this problem we are given the upper value, .67, but we must first enter a lower value.

Based on the theory of the **Standard** Normal Distribution we choose a lower value that will "cut off" a very small amount of the curve thus giving a very small amount of error in our answer.

I choose a lower value of -5   *(This will introduce an error of only .000000287.....)*
                                                Certainly acceptable for most applications.

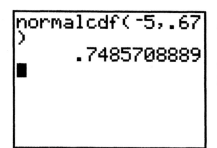

Press: ■-5■ ■.■ ■.67■ ■)■ ENTER

*As can be seen from the screen the probability
is* **.7485708889**

Example 3   **The Normal Distribution**

Let's say we want to use these values from a Restaurant menu:
The mean price of an entrée μ =**\$ 8.93**, with known standard deviation
σ = **\$2.00** and we want to find the probability that an entrée item chosen at random from the menu will fall between **\$10.00** and **\$12.00**.

Press 2nd VARS   (you will see screen below)

We want to choose **"2 : normalcdf ("** , and *press* ENTER

We will need to enter **4** pieces of data and they **must** be entered in this order :
(Lower limit , upper limit , mean , standard deviation)
        Here we will use the actual data not the Z-scores!

For our problem we will use these values **(10 , 12 , 8.93 , 2)** You should be looking at this screen :

Now enter **10** , **12** , **8.93** , **2** **)** ENTER **.2339329725** will be displayed. This is the probability that an item from the menu will fall between **$10.00** and **$12.00** .

Said another way it is the area under the curve between **10.00** and **12.00** of a **Normal Distribution** with **mean = 8.93** and known **standard deviation = 2.00.**

If you want to see a **graph** of this problem we will need to return to the distributions menu and **Arrow right** to " **DRAW** "

[*We will follow the same procedure as before except we will enter 4 pieces of data.*]

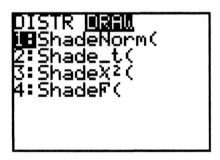

Press ENTER (You will see this screen)

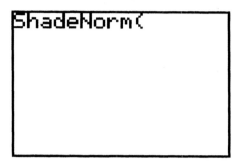

Now we will enter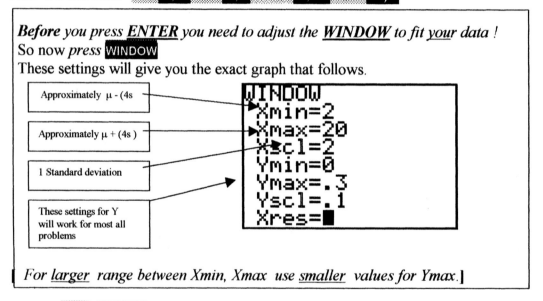

> ***Before*** you press ***ENTER*** you need to adjust the ***WINDOW*** to fit *your* data !
> So now *press* WINDOW
> These settings will give you the exact graph that follows.
>
> | Approximately μ - (4s |
> | Approximately μ + (4s) |
> | 1 Standard deviation |
> | These settings for Y will work for most all problems |
>
> WINDOW
> Xmin=2
> Xmax=20
> Xscl=2
> Ymin=0
> Ymax=.3
> Yscl=.1
> Xres=■
>
> [*For larger range between Xmin, Xmax use smaller values for Ymax.*]

Press 2nd **MODE** to return to this screen:

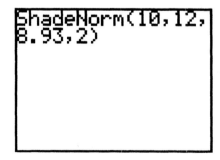

ShadeNorm(10,12,
8.93,2)

Press ENTER (You will see this graph with the appropriate area shaded)

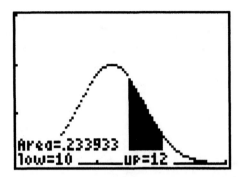

This graph gives us not only the area under the curve but also shows the lower and upper limits.

[Remember to adjust the WINDOW to fit your data whenever you are graphing a problem.]

Example 4   Normal Distribution

Assume that the length of time, x, for a fishing charter is normally distributed with mean = 10 hours and stand deviation = 1.5 hours.
Find the probability that the time spent on an outing is between 8 and 12 hours.

Here we are trying to find the area under the curve so we use "**2:normalcdf**"

Press:

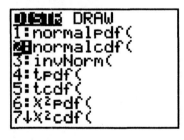

Highlight option "**2:normalcdf** ("

Since we are using the *actual data* in this problem and *not* the z-scores. We will need to enter 4 values. The first 2 will be the same (i.e. lower, upper); however, we now must add 2 more values
...............mean, standard deviation).

Press ENTER

For a Normal Distribution we must enter
Lower , upper , mean , std. Dev.

In that order!

Press: **8** **,** **12** **,** **10** **,** **1.5** **)**

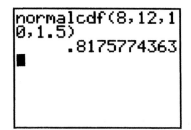

As can be seen from the screen the
probability is **.8175774363**

Note: *the difference between a textbook's answer and the TI-83's answer can be significant.*
Error is introduced whenever one rounds. So rounding at each step in a calculation will introduce significant error by the time all calculations are completed.
It is best to let the calculator carry all decimal places and then you round 1 time at the end.

This may still give a different answer than is in the book. The TI-83Plus displays the more accurate answer in this case.

Finding the Z-score when the area is given

Sometimes we want to find the Z-score when we are given an area under the curve. The "**3:InvNorm(**" option is for just such a problem.

Example 1: Say you want to find the Z-score for the upper 20% of a given population. Since you want the upper 20% that means you are **at** the 80%-ile. On the calculator we will need to go once again to the distributions menu. Go to this screen:

Arrow down to choice "**3 : InvNorm ("**   *Press* ENTER

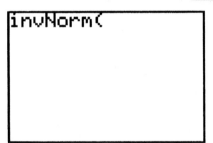

You **must** enter the percentile of the point for which you want the Z-score. We will *press* **.80**   ) ENTER
.8416212335 will be returned. This is the Z-score for the upper 20%.

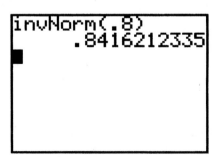

[If you enter "(%-ile , mean , std. Dev.)" the calculator will return the actual value, not the z-score.]

Example 2

Say you know 50% of the area under the curve is between **z** and **–z**. Find **z.**

Since the **Normal Distribution function** is symmetrical it must be that 25% is above the mean and 25% is below the mean. Recall that we **must** enter **the %-ile** of the point for which we desire the Z-score. The mean is in the middle of the curve so its %-ile is 50% and Since 25% is above the mean then we want the Z-score for the 75%-ile. (50% + 25%)

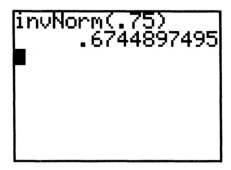

We see that **z = .674**

Example 3

A random variable x has a normal distribution with = 300 and =30.
   a)   Find the probability that x assumes a value more than 1 standard
           deviation from its mean. 2 standard deviations from the mean.
   b)   Find the probability that x assumes a value within 1 standard
           deviation from its mean. 2 standard deviations from the mean.
   c)   Find the value of x that represents the 80th percentile. The 10th
           percentile.

To begin this problem we will use the Distributions Menu.

```
DISTR DRAW
1:normalpdf(
2:normalcdf(
3:invNorm(
4:tpdf(
5:tcdf(
6:X²pdf(
7↓X²cdf(
```

Press: 2nd VARS

Highlight option "**2:normalcdf (**"

To calculate the area under the curve from a **Standard** Normal Distribution you need only enter 2 values: **lower , upper**

Since we want the area outside 2 standard deviations we will calculate the complementary area (e.g. area within 2 standard deviations) and then subtract that result from 1. Giving us the area under the curve that lies outside 2 standard deviations.

Press: ENTER
For our problem we enter **–2** , **2**

(*the negative sign is the gray button*),

Press: - 2 , 2)

Press: ENTER

As can be seen from the screen the Area **within** 2 standard deviations is .954499876 so...........

Therefore the probability that x assumes a value **outside** 2 standard deviations is
1 - .954499876 = **.045500124**

To find the area outside 3 standard deviations follow the same logic.

Press: 2nd ENTER
Arrow left *and replace the 2's with 3's*

Press: ENTER

As can be seen from the screen above the area **within** 3 standard deviations is .9973000656. Therefore the probability that the random variable x takes on a value **outside** 3 standard deviations is 1 - .9973000656 = **.0026999344**

To find the value of x that represents the 80%-ile we will use **3:invNorm**

This time we will enter 3 values: %-ile , mean , standard deviation

Press: 2nd VARS

Highlight option **"3:invNorm ("**

Press: ENTER

Press: **.80** , **300** , **30**)

Press: ENTER

To use this function for this problem you need to enter

the **percentile , mean , std. dev. ,**

in that order, and the calculator will return the <u>actual</u> value --- not the z-value.

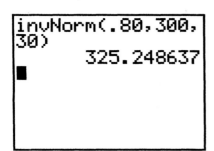

As can be seen from the screen the value corresponding to the 80%-ile is **325.248637**

The Exponential Distribution Function

The Exponential Distribution Function is not a built-in function so we will use a slightly different procedure for calculating the area under the curve.

An Exponential Dist. program is provided in the Problems Section and on the disk.

Let's say we want to know the probability that this transistor will last **at least** 10 years if we know the life of this transistor is distributed Exponentially with a mean life expectancy of 6 years. Here $\mu = 6$, and $x \geq 10$

So our equation would be : $(1 / 6) e^{\wedge}(- x / 6)$

On the calculator you will go to the functions menu. *Press:* Y =

Now we will need to enter the equation

```
Plot1  Plot2  Plot3
\Y1=■
\Y2=
.Y3=
.Y4=
.Y5=
.Y6=
.Y7=
```

Press   (1   ÷   6   )   2nd   LN   (-)   X,T,θ,n   ÷   6   )
(you will see this text appearing on screen as you type)

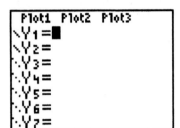

```
Plot1  Plot2  Plot3
\Y1◤(1/6)e^( -X/6
)
\Y2=
.Y3=
.Y4=
.Y5=
.Y6=
```

Now we need to adjust the WINDOW to fit our data. So *press:* WINDOW

```
WINDOW
 Xmin=■
 Xmax=48
 Xscl=6
 Ymin=0
 Ymax=.16666666...
 Yscl=0
 Xres=1
```

Xmin = 0 , Xmax = 8μ , Xscl = μ , Ymin = 0 , Ymax = 1/μ, Yscl = < 1/μ
These settings will always give you a nice view of the Exponential graph.

Now on to the graph. *Press:* GRAPH   (you will see this graph)

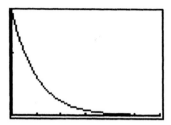

To find the area under the curve past **x =10** we will need to go to the **Function's**
Calculations menu. So *press:* ▓▓▓ **TRACE** (this screen will appear)

Arrow down to " 7 : { f (x) dx "
[*This choice will integrate the function between two points*]
Next, *press* **ENTER**

[Since we wanted **x ≥ 10** , <u>**10**</u> will be the lower limit and <u>**48**</u> will
be our upper limit. <u>**48**</u> because our graph window only goes up to **48**]

Now press **10 ENTER 48 ENTER**   (this screen will appear)

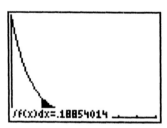

This screen shows us that the area under the curve past **10** is **.18854014**
So the probability that a transistor with a known life expectancy of **6** years
will last at least **10** years $\approx$ **0.189.**

   (1 – the Integral 0 to 10) = (1 – 0.8111244) = 0.1887 ≈ 0.189 .
[*Recall that to clear the screen after shading you will need to go to the* **"DRAW"** *menu,*
Press **2nd PRGM** *"1 : ClrDraw " will be highlighted, press* **ENTER**]

Simple random samples

Many times you will need to choose a random sample from a population. You can of course use the random number tables found at the back of the book or let the calculator "choose" for you.

Say we want to randomly select 5 people from a class of 20 for a particular study project. First we assign the numbers 1 – 20 to the people in the class. Next we go to the Probability menu on the calculator.

Press: **MATH** **Arrow left** to " **PRB** ". Highlight **"5 : randInt "**

```
MATH NUM CPX PRB
1:rand
2:nPr
3:nCr
4: !
5:randInt(
6:randNorm(
7:randBin(
```

Press: **ENTER** (see screen below)

```
randInt(█
```

Now you **must** enter these numbers in this order **(smallest number , largest number , sample size)**

For our problem we will *press* **1** **,** **20** **,** **5** **)** **ENTER**

Five numbers will be displayed inside set braces . These are the **5** randomly selected people for our study group.

My group will be persons numbered   **{ 4 8 3 5 18 }** .

Of course your 5 numbers will most likely be different.

Confidence Intervals

When calculating a confidence interval there are three one sample choices on
 the calculator.   1. **Z-Interval**
2. **T-Interval**
3. **Proportions**

Example 1

Say we want to develop a **95%** confidence interval for the population mean
from a sample size of **35** where we know the sample mean is **100** and the
population deviation is **12**. For this problem we want **Z-Interval**

On the calculator we will choose **"7 :Zinterval"** from the **"TESTS"** menu.
Now go to the **"TESTS"** menu
press **STAT** (this screen will appear)

```
EDIT CALC TESTS
1:Edit…
2:SortA(
3:SortD(
4:ClrList
5:SetUpEditor
```

Arrow right to " TEST " . Arrow down to " 7 : ZInterval " (see below left)

```
EDIT CALC TESTS
1:Z-Test…
2:T-Test…
3:2-SampZTest…
4:2-SampTTest…
5:1-PropZTest…
6:2-PropZTest…
7↓ZInterval…
```

```
ZInterval
Inpt:Data Stats
σ:12
x̄:100
n:35
C-Level:.95
Calculate
```

Press **ENTER** (you will see upper right screen)

You must highlight either **"Data"** or " **Stats"** and *press:* **ENTER**

If you choose " Data" the calculator will read the data from **LIST** .
If you choose "Stats" then you will have to enter the statistics yourself.
For this problem we want to highlight   " **Stats"**
Next **You** must set σ : **12**,   mean : **100**, n : **35**, C-Level : **.95**

Now highlight **"Calculate"** and *press* ENTER

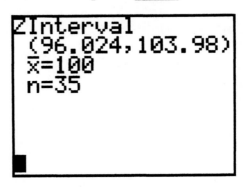

As you can see our confidence interval is **(96.024 , 103.98)** This means
that repeated samples from this population will give a mean value between
96.024 and **103.98** **95%** of the time.

Example 2   Confidence Intervals

Say we want to report the 99% confidence level of the mean for this
simple random sample **{ 7 , 7, 8, 9, 7, 10, 6, 8, 9, 9 }** taken from a **known
Normal Population** of 120 where the **population** standard deviation is **1.2**

For this problem we want a Z-Interval since we have a known sigma.
First we will enter our data into **List1**.   (see screen below)

L1	L2	L3 1
7	------	------
7		
8		
9		
7		
10		
6		
L1(1)=7		

Next we need to once again go to the **TEST** menu . *Press* STAT

Arrow right to "**TEST**" and highlight "**7 : ZInterval**"

Press ENTER (left screen will appear)

This time we want to choose "**Data**" So highlight "**Data**" and *press* ENTER
(*When you press* **ENTER** *the screen will automatically change* to lower right)

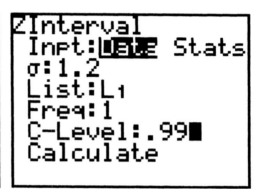

You will need to set the σ to **1.2** and the "**C-Level** " to **.99**

And make sure the **List : L1** (our data is in list1)

Now highlight "**Calculate**" and *press* ENTER (you will see this screen)

```
ZInterval
 (7.0225,8.9775)
 x̄=8
 Sx=1.247219129
 n=10
```

We can see that the **interval estimate** using α = **.01** is **(7.0225 , 8.9775)**

Again, this means that with repeated samples we will get a mean value
between **7.0225** and **8.9775,   99 %** of the time.

Example 3   Confidence Intervals

Lets say we want to calculate a **95 %** confidence interval for a population
mean from some sample data. The sample std. dev. is **6** , and the sample
mean is **55.** The sample size is **15.**
 In this problem we should use a **T-interval** not a Z-interval.
(*we have a sample < 30* , *we do* **not** *know the population standard deviation*)

On the calculator go to the **"TESTS"** menu.
Press STAT
Arrow right to "**TESTS**" and down to " **8 : TInterval** " (see screen below)

Press ENTER (this screen will appear)

Once again we must choose **"Stats".** *Press* ENTER

Arrow down and change the settings on your screen to match these.
    X : 55 ,   Sx : 6 ,   n : 15 ,   C-Level : .95

Highlight "**Calculate**" and *press* ENTER. (you will see this screen)

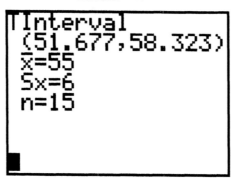

As we can see from the screen above the **95%** confidence interval is
(51.677 , 58.323). This means that from repeated samples of this population
will get a mean value between **51.677** an **58.323** **95%** of the time.

Example 4   Confidence Intervals

The duration (in minutes) for a sample of **18 OSCAR** telephone registrations
is shown below: (begin by typing the data into **L1**)

2.1   4.8   5.5   10.4   3.3   3.5   4.8   5.8   5.3
2.8   3.6   5.9   6.6   7.8   10.5   7.5   6.0   4.5

What is the point estimate of the population mean? Compute the **98%**
confidence interval for the population mean.

For this problem we need to use a **T-interval** since the sample is less than **30**
and of unknown distribution with unknown sigma.

On the calculator we want to go to the **"TESTS"**   menu. So *press* STAT
Arrow right to " TESTS" and down to **"8 : TInterval"**

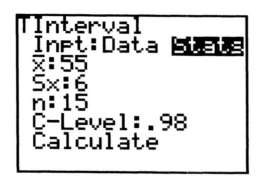

Press ENTER   (see screen above)

Next we want to highlight **"Data"** and *press* ENTER

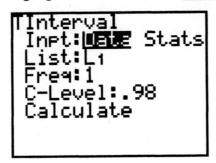

Now the only thing left to change is the "**C-Level :**".

Make sure you change **"C-Level :"** to ___ **.98**
then highlight **"Calculate "** and *press* ENTER
(you will see this screen)

```
TInterval
 (4.178,7.0109)
 x̄=5.594444444
 Sx=2.34105864
 n=18
```

This shows us the **98%** confidence interval is **(4.178, 7.0109).** Once again this means that repeated samples of this population will yield a mean value between **4.178** and **7.0109**   **98%** of the time.

Interval Estimation of a Population Proportion

We can satisfy the requirements of the Central Limit Theorem and develop the interval estimation of a proportion of a population by using z-values as long as we use large samples. For most applications we consider a sample large as long as $np > 5$, and $n(1 - p) > 5.$

Example 1

A simple random sample of **200** students at a West Florida University reveals that only **19%** study Statistics more than **2** hours a week at home. Using a **95%** confidence level provide an interval estimate of the proportion of the population of students who study more than **2** hours a week at home.

For this problem $p = .19$, $n = 200$,   and $E(x) = .19* 200 = 38$

On the calculator we want to go to the **"TESTS"** menu. *Press* STAT
Arrow right to **"TESTS"** and **Arrow up** to **"A : 1 – PropZInt..."**
Press ENTER (you will see this screen)

```
1-PropZInt
 x:38
 n:200
 C-Level:.95
 Calculate
```

Adjust your settings to match these on the screen. **Arrow down** to
"Calculate"   *Press* ENTER   (you will see this screen)

```
1-PropZInt
 (.13563,.24437)
 p̂=.19
 n=200
```

As you can see from the screen the interval estimate of the proportion of the population of the students who study more than **2** hours a week at home is:
(.136 , .244)

Hypothesis Testing

Just a reminder here: The equal sign always goes with **Ho.**
We always test **Ha,**
and we reject **Ho** if $p < \alpha$.

Example 1   (One Tailed Z-Test)

A Casino in Biloxi claims that at least **40,000** people, give or take **1000** people visit their Casino every week. A random survey of **30** different weeks shows a sample mean of **39,600** people. Using a **0.02** level of significance, test whether or not there is sufficient evidence to reject their claim.

For this problem a **Z-Test** is appropriate. **(known σ)**

    Ho : $\mu \geq 40,000$
    Ha : $\mu < 40,000$ so   We will reject **Ho** if $p < .02$

On the calculator we start from the "**TESTS**" menu.

Press STAT
Arrow right to Highlight "**TESTS**"
" **1 : Z-Test…**" should be highlighted then *press* ENTER (see screen below)

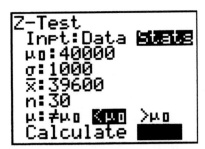

If we want to enter the data ourselves we choose "Stats"
If we want the calculator to read from the Lists we choose "Data"

Arrow down and change settings to match this screen. (see screen above)

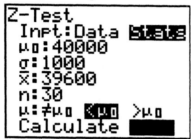

Highlight "**Calculate**" and *press* ENTER (this screen will appear)

```
Z-Test
 μ<40000
 z=-2.19089023
 P=.0142298183
 x̄=39600
 n=30
```

We can see from the screen that the **"p"** value is **0.014** which is less than **0.02,** so we reject **Ho**.

Example 2 (Two Tailed Z-Test)

A particular bottle filling process is designed to fill bottles with a mean of **12** Fl. Oz. This process has a standard deviation of **.07** Fl. Oz. Quantities above or below this amount are undesirable.

A sample of **10** bottles is taken to determine if the process is within limits. These are the sample volumes:

11.6   12.1   11.9   12.8   11.9   12.0   12.4   11.6   11.8   12.3

Using a **0.05** level of significance, test to see if the sample results indicate the filling process is functioning properly.

For this problem: **Ho:** $\mu = 12$

                        Ha : $\mu \neq 12$

On the calculator we will first enter the data into LIST1.

Next we will go to the " **TESTS** " menu.

Press **STAT**

Arrow right to "**TESTS**"(you will see this screen)

Highlight "**1 : Z – Test…**" *Press* **ENTER** (this screen will appear)

Once again we must choose either "**Data**" or "**Stats**"

This time we will choose "**Data**".

Arrow down and change the settings to fit our problem.

$\mu = 12$, $\sigma = .07$.   *Recall we always test* **Ha.**

Highlight **"Calculate"** and *press* `ENTER`   (you will see this screen)

```
Z-Test
 μ≠12
 z=1.807015806
 P=.070759705
 x̄=12.04
 Sx=.3747591819
 n=10
```

From the screen we see the **"p"** value is .071 which is greater than **0.05;** therefore, we **can not** reject Ho

Example 3   (One Tailed T-Test)

A local Flea market business decided to sell their original "Salsa in a jar".
The process of "canning" the salsa is designed to produce a mean of at least
120
jars of salsa per batch. Quantities under this amount are undesirable.
A sample of **10** batches shows the following numbers of jars of salsa:

   108   118   120   122   119   113   124   122   120   123

Using $\alpha = $ **0.05** , test to see if the sample results indicate the "canning"
process is providing the desired number of jars.

For this problem we have unknown sigma so we need to use a **"T=Test"**

For this problem   **Ho : $\mu \geq$ 120**
                    Ha : $\mu <$ 120,   so we will reject **Ho** if **p < .05**

To begin this problem we first enter the sample data into "**List1**".
Then, *Press* **STAT**   (this screen will appear)

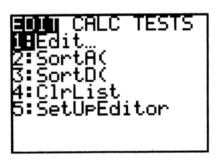

Arrow right to **"TESTS"** next Arrow down to **"2 : T-Test..."**

Press **ENTER**   (you will see this screen)

Once again we must choose between **"Data"** and **"Stats"**

We will choose **"Data"** for this problem because we have entered the actual data into **list1.**

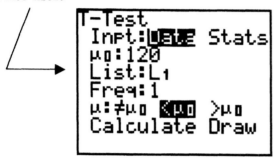

Change the other settings on your calculator to match the screen above.

Press ENTER

Arrow down to highlight **"Calculate"**

Press ENTER   (you will see this screen)

```
T-Test
µ<120
t=-.7053278934
P=.2492266222
x̄=118.9
Sx=4.931756505
n=10
```

You can see from the screen that the p-value is **.24**, which is **not** less than **.05** Therefore we **can not** reject Ho.

   Our conclusion would be: At α = 0.05 there is not sufficient evidence to reject the claim that the mean number of jars produced is at least **120.**

Example 4   (Two Tailed T-Test)

Consider the following hypothesis test: **Ho** : $\mu = 20$

Ha : $\mu \neq 20$

Data from a sample of **10** items gave the following results:

Sample mean = **21.02**, s = **1.65**.

At what level of α would you reject **Ho**?

A **T-Test** is needed in this situation since we have a small sample with unknown population deviation, σ.

Recall: we reject **Ho** if $p < \alpha$; therefore, **we** need to determine the **p-value** for this problem and then we will have our answer.

If **alpha** is any number greater than our **p-value** then we would reject **Ho**.

On the calculator go to the **"Tests"** menu.

Arrow right to **"TESTS"** and **Arrow down** to **"2 : T – Test…"**

Press ENTER (see screen below)

```
T-Test
 Inpt:Data
 µ0:20
 x̄:21.02
 Sx:1.65
 n:10
 µ: ≠µ0  <µ0  >µ0
 Calculate Draw
```

Match previous settings on your calculator.

Arrow down to **"Calculate"** and *press* ENTER (this screen will appear)

```
T-Test
 µ≠20
 t=1.954862554
 p=.082321212
 x̄=21.02
 Sx=1.65
 n=10
```

We can see that the **p-value** is **.082** As stated earlier we reject Ho if $p < \alpha$,

So for any **alpha** greater than **.082**, we would reject **Ho** ☺

Testing a claim about a proportion

Researchers who study hot pepper's active ingredient capsaicin report that at least **70%** of the people who add capsaicin to their diet burn an extra **50** calories per day. A study at The Oxford Polytechnic Institute found that of the **72** people who consumed identical diets with capsaicin **44** showed an extra loss of **50** calories per day. Test this claim using $\alpha = .02$.

For our problem : **Ho: p $\geq$ .70** ,

                       Ha : p < .70 ,   so we reject **Ho** if **p < .02**

Recall : x = n*p   so our x = 72 * (44/72) = 44.

On the calculator we will once again go to the **"TESTS"** menu.
Press STAT

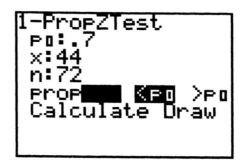

Arrow right to **"TESTS"** and **Arrow down** to **"5 : 1-PropZTest…"**
Press ENTER (this screen will appear)

Remember we always test Ha. Highlight " < p_0 " and *press* ENTER
Next Arrow down to "Calculate" and *press* ENTER (you will see this screen)

```
1-PropZTest
 prop<.7
 z=-1.6459024
 p=.0498919115
 p̂=.6111111111
 n=72
```

As you can see from the screen the p-value is **.049** which is **not < .02** therefore we **can not** reject **Ho.**
So we can not refute the claim at the alpha = **.02** level that capsaicin causes the burning of an extra **50** calories per day in **70%** of the people who ingest it.

Inferences about Two Populations

We use s1, s2 for σ1, σ2 since the point estimate for σ (x1-x2) using s1, and s2 is considered a good estimator with large samples.

Example 1 (Two Sample Z-Interval)

Consider the results shown below for independent random samples taken from two populations :

	Sample 1	Sample 2
	$n_1 = 50$	$n_2 = 35$
	$x_1 = 13.6$	$x_2 = 11.6$
	$s_1 = 2.2$	$s_2 = 3.0$

Give the point estimate of the difference, and provide a **95%** confidence interval for the difference between the means.
We will start from the **"TESTS"** menu .

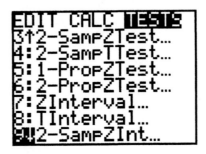

Press STAT (see screen below)

Arrow right to **"TESTS"** and down to choice **"9 : 2 SampZInt…"**

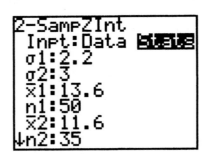

Press ENTER (you will see this screen)

Once again you must choose **"Data"** or **"Stats"**. We will choose **"Stats"**.

Change your settings to match the settings on these screens:
Arrow down and highlight **"Calculate"** (you will see this screen)

```
2-SampZInt
↑σ2:3
 x̄1:13.6
 n1:50
 x̄2:11.6
 n2:35
 C-Level:.95
█
```

[Recall we are entering s1, s2 for σ1, σ2.]

Press ENTER (this screen will appear)

```
2-SampZInt
 (.83396,3.166)
 x̄1=13.6
 x̄2=11.6
 n1=50
 n2=35
```

As you can see from the screen the **95%** confidence interval for the difference of the means is **(.83396 , 3.166)**.

The point estimate can also be calculated from this screen .
It is **13.6 – 11.6 = 2.0**

Example 2   (Two Sample T-Interval)

The following results were gathered independently from two different colleges in Florida. The number of hours spent studying for the Statistics Final Exam. are shown below:

	College 1	College 2
	$n1 = 10$	$n2 = 8$
	$x1 = 22.5$	$x2 = 20.1$
	$s1 = 2.5$	$s2 = 2.0$

Give the point estimate of the difference between the two means, and develop a **98%** confidence interval for the difference between the two means.

For this problem we will use a two sample T-interval since **n1<30, n2<30.** Again we will start from the **"TESTS"** menu.

```
EDIT CALC TESTS
4↑2-SampTTest…
5:1-PropZTest…
6:2-PropZTest…
7:ZInterval…
8:TInterval…
9:2-SampZInt…
0:2-SampTInt…
```

Press STAT **Arrow right** to **"TESTS"** and choose **"0: 2-SampTInt…"**

Press ENTER

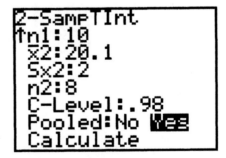

Once again we will highlight **"Stats"** and *press* ENTER (see left screen)

There is one **new** line on this menu.

It is " Pooled : No   Yes "

Pooled or non-pooled is based on equal or not equal population variances. There is a test for this assumption: *see page 97 for a full description.*

The F Test : Ho : var(pop1) = var(pop2) >>> $s_1^2 = s_2^2$ (equal)

Ha : var(pop1) ≠ var(pop2) >> $s_1^2 ≠ s_2^2$ (not equal)

This test can be performed on the TI-83PLUSPlus.

Go to the tests menu. *Press* `STAT` and choose option "**D: 2-SampFTest...**"

You will have the same choices as with any of the tests.

Highlight **Stats** for this problem: since we are entering the statistics ourselves.

Match your screen to this problem's statistics and

ALWAYS highlight σ1: "≠ σ2"

Press `ENTER`

Arrow down to calculate and *press* `ENTER`

As you can see from your screen the p-value is .5694 .

We would reject Ho only if $p < \alpha$. *At 98% CI the* $\alpha = .02$.

As this p-value is **not** less than α we can **not** reject Ho.

Therefore, we should assume equal variances which means we will choose **"pooled"**

Highlight **"Yes"** , and *press* `ENTER`

Arrow down to "Calculate" and *press* `ENTER` (this screen will appear)

```
2-SampTInt
 (-.412,5.212)
 df=16
 x̄1=22.5
 x̄2=20.1
 Sx1=2.5
↓Sx2=2
■
```

As you can see from the screen the Interval estimate of the difference is **(-.412 , 5.212).** We can also calculate the point estimate of the difference from this screen. It is **22.5 – 20.1** which is **2.5**

Example 3   Paired T-Interval

An study is conducted to compare the money generated at a High-school Football game before and after a favorite coach is replaced. Calculate the 95% confidence for the difference between the money generated before and after the coach is replaced.

game	before	after
1	29,300	28,800
2	41,500	41,600
3	40,400	39,800
4	38,500	38,500
5	43,500	42,600
6	37,800	38,000
7	69,500	69,200
8	41,200	40,100
9	38,400	38,200
10	59,200	58,500

To perform a Paired Difference Confidence Interval on the calculator first enter the data into List 1 and List 2.

I will enter *before* into List 1 and *after* into List 2. The next step is to create List 3 which will be (List 1 - List 2).

Enter your data into List 1 and List 2.

L1	L2	**L3**	3
29300	28800	-----	
41500	41600		
40400	39800		
38500	38500		
43500	42600		
37800	38000		
69500	69200		

L3 =

*For matched pair calculations you **MUST** enter the data in the **EXACT** order it is given.*

After you have entered all the data Arrow up and highlight the L3 itself (not the top line of the data)

Press: ([2nd] [1] - [2nd] [2]) [ENTER]

You will see the expression scroll across the bottom of your screen.
List 3 will be **created** as you press: ENTER

List 3 is the difference between List 1 and List 2.

Next *Press* [STAT]

```
EDIT CALC TESTS
2↑T-Test...
3:2-SampZTest...
4:2-SampTTest...
5:1-PropZTest...
6:2-PropZTest...
7:ZInterval...
8:TInterval...
```

Arrow left *to* TESTS *and* **Arrow Down** *to* " 8: TInterval..."

press [ENTER]

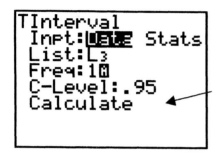

Notice we choose **data** *and we are using* **List 3**

The problem ask for the 95% CI.

Don't forget to enter it in decimal format.

Arrow Down to **Calculate** *and*

press ENTER

```
TInterval
 (89.096,710.9)
 x̄=400
 Sx=434.6134937
 n=10

■
```

As can be seen from the screen the 95% CI is **$(89.10 , 710.90)** rounded to the nearest penny.

Hypothesis Test About the Difference of Two Populations

Just as before, the equal sign always goes with **Ho.**
We always test **Ha,**   and we reject **Ho** if $p < \alpha$.

Example 1   (Two Sample Z-Test)

The following results are for independent random samples taken from two
Populations. Consider the following hypothesis test:

		Ho: $\mu 1 - \mu 2 \le 0$
Sample 1	Sample 2	**Ha:** $\mu 1 - \mu 2 > 0.$
n1 = 40	n2 = 50	
x1 = 25.2	x2 = 22.8	
s1 = 5.2	s2 = 6.0	

Using alpha = **.05**, test the hypothesis. What is your conclusion?
For this problem we will use a **Z-test** and we will reject **Ho** if $p < .05$
Start from the **"TESTS"** menu.
Press **STAT Arrow right** to **"TESTS"**
 and **Arrow down** to **"3 : 2-SampZTest…"**

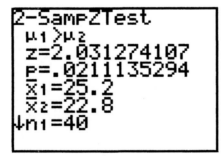

Press **ENTER**
Choose **"Stats"** and press **ENTER**.

Next, match the settings on your
calculator to those on the above screen.
Be sure you choose the alternative test
 " $> \mu 2$ "

Arrow down to **"Calculate"** and *press* **ENTER**

```
2-SampZTest
 µ1 >µ2
 z=2.031274107
 p=.0211135294
 x1=25.2
 x2=22.8
↓n1=40
```

From the screen the p-value = **.02** which is **< .05** therefore we **reject Ho**

Example 2   (Two Sample T-Test)

Sample of Final Exam scores from two statistics classes with different instructors provided the following results:

	Instructor A	Instructor B
	$n1 = 12$	$n2 = 15$
	$x1 = 72$	$x2 = 79$
	$s1 = 8$	$s2 = 10$

Using $\alpha = .05$, test whether these data are sufficient to conclude that the population mean grades differ for the two instructors.

First we need to develop the null and alternative hypothesis.

Ho : $\mu1 - \mu2 = 0$

Ha : $\mu1 - \mu2 \neq 0$ and we will reject Ho if p < .05

For this problem we will use a T-test. Start from the **"TESTS"** menu.
Press **STAT** **Arrow right** to **"TESTS"** and **Arrow down** to
"4 : 2-SampTTest…"
Press **ENTER** (see screen below)

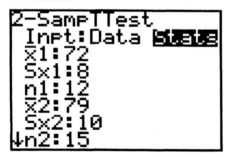

Choose **"Stats"** and *press* **ENTER**
Next, match the settings on your calculator to those on the above screen.
Be sure you highlight the alternative test " $\neq$ "

Now we need to calculate the **F Test statistic**.
This is because we have to choose Pooled or Not Pooled

To calculate the **F Test statistic** by hand:

F = 10^2 ÷ 8^2 = 100 / 64 = 1.5625 now consult a F-table

(*or use your TI as we did in example 2, 2-tailed T-Interval above*)

```
2-SampTTest
↑n1:12
 x̄2:79
 Sx2:10
 n2:15
 μ1:≠μ2 <μ2 >μ2
 Pooled:No Yes
 Calculate Draw
```

In either case we can assume equal variances so highlight **"Yes"**
Arrow down to **"Calculate"** and *press* ENTER (see screen below)

```
2-SampTTest
 μ1≠μ2
 t=-1.970151153
 p=.0599932276
 df=25
 x̄1=72
↓x̄2=79
■
```

As you can see from the screen above the p-value = **.06** which is not less
than **.05** therefore we **can not reject Ho** .

In conclusion we must say that at the alpha = .05 level there is not sufficient
evidence to claim that the mean test scores between the two instructors differ.

Example 3   (Two Proportion Population Test)

The following results are for independent random samples taken from two populations:

	Sample 1	Sample 2
	$n1 = 200$	$n2 = 300$
	$p_1 = .22$	$p_2 = .18$

Using alpha = **.05**, test to see if the two population proportion's are the same.

On the calculator we once again go to the **"TESTS"** menu.
Press STAT

Next **Arrow right** to **"TESTS"** and **Arrow down** to **"6 : 2-PropZTest..."**
(left screen)

 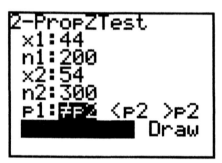

Press ENTER   (right screen)
Enter your values from the problem.
We will test " ≠ "   **Arrow down** to **"Calculate"**

Press ENTER(this screen will appear)

```
2-PropZTest
 P1≠P2
 z=1.103810585
 P=.2696753953
 p̂1=.22
 p̂2=.18
↓p̂=.196
```

As you can see from the screen the p-value is **.270** which is **not** < **.05** so we do **not** reject **Ho.**

There is not sufficient evidence at the α = **.05** level to reject the claim that these two proportions are the same.

Correlation & Regression

The **TI-83PLUS** is the perfect tool for calculating the Pearson Product Moment Coefficient(**r**), and for calculating the Legendre Linear Regression Equation
(**y= aX+b**).   [*Where **a** = the slope of the regression line and*
* **b** = the y-intercept of the regression line*.]

Recall that the correlation coefficient is a number which describes the strength and direction of the relationship between two variables.

In simple relationships there are only two variables and the correlation coefficient ranges between :
 (perfect negative correlation) **–1** <<<< **r** <<<< **+1** (perfect positive correlation)

with **r = 0** being **no** linear correlation.

If there is a linear correlation then a Legendre Linear Regression Equation (also called the line of best fit) will give us the model used to predict results between the two variables.

A **Scatter Plot** of the data should always be done first as it provides an excellent **visual method** for determining whether or not a correlation exists; however, it is highly **subjective**.

There is a more **objective test** for determining whether or not two variables are **linearly** related.
For this test we must develop a **Null** and **Alternative Hypothesis,**

Ho: There is no Linear relationship
Ha: There is a Linear relationship

Here we **reject Ho if**   **r > c.v.** or **r < -c.v.**
[c.v. is the critical value found from the Pearson Product Moment Coefficient tables* using α and (n – 2) degrees of freedom]

OR
there is a test on the TI-83Plus for this.
It is the Linear Regression T-Test, **"LinRegTTest..."**
For the calculator test we would, as always, reject Ho if $p < \alpha$.

Example 1   (Correlation)

A College Algebra instructor suspects there is a relationship between *the number of previous courses a student has had using the graphing calculator* **and** *the final average of the student in the current Algebra course.* The data is as follows:

Number of previous Courses with calculator	1	2	2	0	1	1	0	2	1	1
Final average in Algebra	90	98	95	86	85	94	80	90	92	95

Draw a Scatter Plot, compute the correlation coefficient (**r**), state Ho and Ha, test the Hypothesis using $\alpha = 0.05$, and give the conclusion.

For this section and the one that follows we must turn "on" the diagnostic capabilities of the calculator.

Press `2nd` `0` **Arrow down** to **"DiagnosticOn"** *Press* `ENTER` `ENTER`

Next, begin by entering the data into the calculator. *Press* `STAT`
(you will see this screen)

```
EDIT CALC TESTS
1:Edit…
2:SortA(
3:SortD(
4:ClrList
5:SetUpEditor
```

Press `ENTER` (the lower left screen appears) ***Always start from a clear list.***

Now ENTER the **X** values into **LIST1** and the **Y** values into **LIST2**. *remember to press ENTER after each entry* (you should be looking at top right screen)

To see a Scatter Plot of this data we will go to the **STAT PLOT** menu so

Press 2nd Y = . (this screen will appear)
Press ENTER

Make sure **"ON"** is highlighted and
press ENTER
Next **Arrow down** to "**Scatter Plot**" and
press ENTER
Make sure **Xlist : L1 , Ylist : L2**
You may choose any **"Mark"** you desire.
 I will choose ▣

You can now press ZOOM 9 *to have the
calculator automatically adjust the window to
the data. If you choose ZOOM 9 you will need
to extend the window settings to finish this
problem.*

Now we adjust the **WINDOW** to fit the data. Press WINDOW
For our data **Xmin= -1, Xmax= 3, Xscl= 1, Ymin= 75, Ymax= 100, Yscl= 5.**

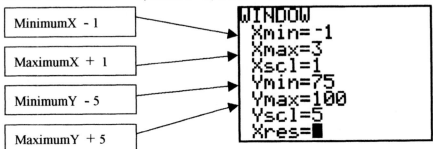

Next *press* GRAPH (you will see this screen)

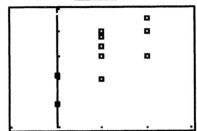

As you can see from the screen there appears to be a positive correlation.
Now to determine the correlation coefficient we will go to the Statistical
Calculations Menu .

For this problem our Null and Alternative Hypothesis are as follows:
  Ho: there is no linear relationship
  Ha: there is a linear relationship

Press STAT (you will see this screen)

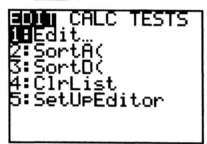

Arrow right to "CALC" and then highlight "4 : LinReg (aX + b) "
(the screen will automatically change to the screen below left)

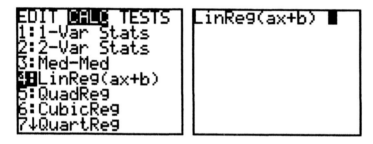

Press ENTER *by default the calculator will choose* LIST1 *and* LIST2 so

Press ENTER (you will see this screen)

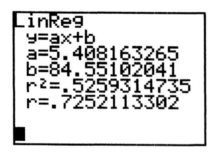

*If you are not using LIST1, LIST2 then you must enter the
X-LIST, Y-LIST in that order before you press ENTER!*

As you see from the screen the Pearson Product Moment Coefficient is **r =
0.725**

If you do not see " r " on your screen you must turn on the Diagnostic.

For our problem the critical value from the tables* is **c.v. = 0.632**

[*We are using $\alpha = 0.05$ and there are [10 − 2] = 8 degrees of freedom*]

Since our **r = 0.725 > 0.632** we **reject Ho.**
Therefore there is sufficient evidence at alpha = .05 to reject the claim of **no** linear relationship.

Using the Linear Regression T-Test found on the calculator

First *press* STAT   **Arrow left** to **"TESTS"**   then **Arrow up** to **"E : LinRegTTest…"**
Press ENTER Make sure you enter the appropriate list and frequency.

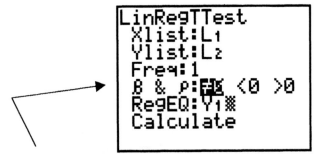

Always choose "≠"
Arrow down to "Calculate" and *press* ENTER (see screens below)

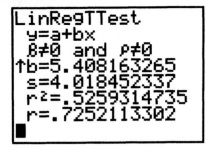

As you can see from the screen our p-value is **0.176** which **is less** than **0.05**, therefore we should **reject** Ho.

You will notice the calculator also gives the Correlation Coefficient (r), the T test statistic, and the coefficients to the equation for "the line of best fit"

Example 2 (Regression)

The paired data below consist of the total weights (in pounds) of discarded garbage and the sizes of households.

Total weight	10.8	19.9	27.6	38.1	27.9	21.9	21.8	49.3	33.3	35.5
Size	2	3	3	6	4	2	1	5	6	4

Draw a Scatter Plot, Give the regression equation, Predict the family size if **32** pounds of garbage is discarded, and predict the pounds of discarded garbage for a household of size **8**. On the calculator we begin by entering data into the **Lists**

Press STAT

Press ENTER (this screen will appear)

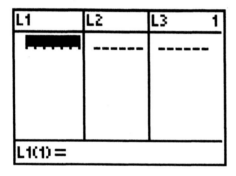

You should enter your **X**-values into **LIST1** and the **Y**-values into **LIST2**.

To see a Scatter Plot we go to **STAT PLOT**. *Press* 2nd Y =

Press ENTER Next make sure **"ON"** is highlighted and *press* ENTER

Arrow down and highlight **"Scatter Plot"** (see right screen)
Make sure **Xlist : L1, Ylist : L2** you may choose any "mark" you desire.

Next we must adjust the **WINDOW** to fit the data so *press* WINDOW
OR you may *press* ZOOM ▨9

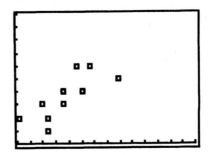

Match your settings to screen above. Now *press* GRAPH (see screen above)
   We see there appears to be a positive correlation.

*When you are predicting values it is a good idea to increase the domain and range of the window **beyond** the actual data.*
This is still necessary even when you are using "ZOOM 9 ")

Now to determine the regression equation we go to the **Statistical Calculations Menu** so *press* STAT (lower left screen will appear)

```
EDIT CALC TESTS       EDIT CALC TESTS
1:Edit…                1:1-Var Stats
2:SortA(               2:2-Var Stats
3:SortD(               3:Med-Med
4:ClrList              4:LinReg(ax+b)
5:SetUpEditor          5:QuadReg
                       6:CubicReg
                       7↓QuartReg
```

Arrow right to **"CALC"** and down to **"4 : LinReg (aX+b) "** (see above)
Press ENTER (lower left screen will appear)

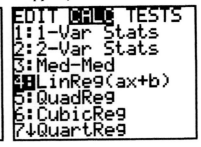

Since the default setting will use **LIST1** and **LIST2** we can now *press* ENTER
As you can see from the screen the regression equation is **Y = .119X + .183**

We also see the correlation coefficient **r = .762**, and one other piece of information **r^2 = .580**.

This "**r^2**" is called the **Coefficient of Determination.**

It is the **ratio** of *the explained variation* **to** *the amount of total variation*.

Also the **Coefficient of Non-determination** can be found by subtracting **r^2** from **1.000**. It is: **1.000 – 0.580 = 0.420**

You may be wondering just how closely this **"best fit line"** matches our data. We can graph the regression line on top of our data by following these several steps:

First *press* Y = (this screen will appear)

Now *press* VARS (you will see this screen)

Arrow down to "**5 : Statistics…**" and *press* ENTER (see screen below)

Arrow right and highlight **"EQ"**.   **"1 : RegEQ"** should also be highlighted.
Press ENTER (this screen will appear)

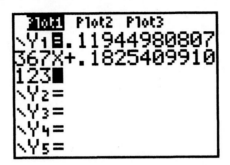

As you can see the regression equation has been pasted into the function line.
Now *press* GRAPH (the regression equation will be graphed along with the
original data)

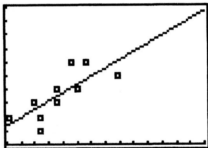

You can find the predicted values from this screen.

We want to find the size of a family if **32 lbs** of garbage was discarded.
Now we go to the **Function Calculations Menu.**
Press 2nd TRACE

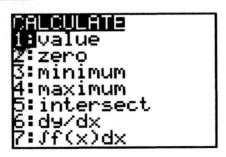

"1 : value" should be highlighted then *press* 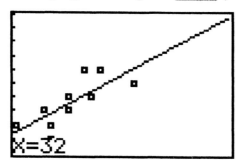 ENTER (this screen will appear)

We simply enter the value **32** and *press* ENTER (this screen will appear)

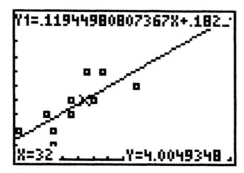

As you can see from the screen we would predict a family of size **4** .

Lastly, we want to find the pounds of garbage discarded if the family size is **8**. Since we know **"Y"** (lbs of garbage) we need to enter that information into the function line (**Y=**).

So press **Y =**   **Arrow down** to"**Y2=**"   Enter **8**

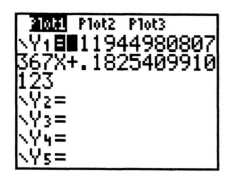
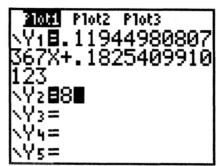

Next *press* GRAPH (this screen will appear)

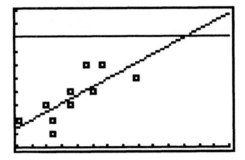

The intersection point <u>is</u> our solution.

Again *press* 2nd TRACE (this screen will reappear)

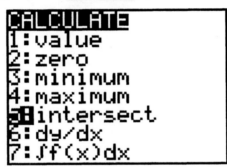

Arrow down to "5 : intersect" and *press* ENTER (see screen below)

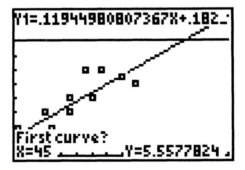

Notice that at the top of the screen the regression equation is displayed.

Press: **ENTER** (you will see this screen)

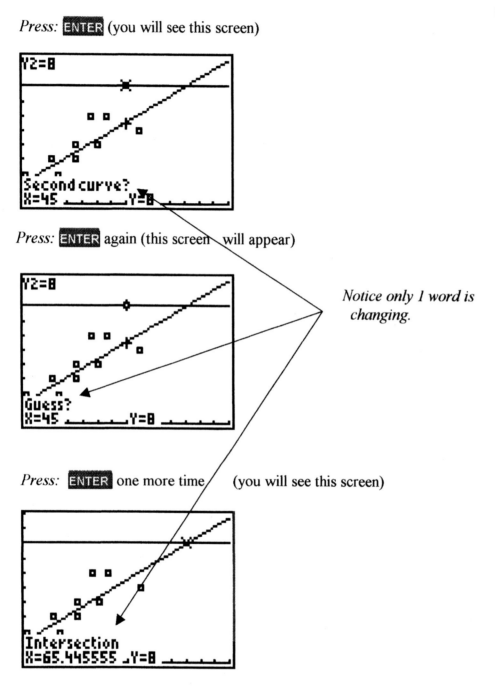

Press: **ENTER** again (this screen will appear)

Notice only 1 word is changing.

Press: **ENTER** one more time (you will see this screen)

As you can see the intersection point is **X=65.4, Y= 8,** so for our problem the predicted amount of garbage from a family of **8** would be **65.4 lbs.**

ANOVA

ANOVA is an acronym for Analysis Of Variance.

It is a method for comparing 3 or more means by using multiple F Tests.

For ANOVA we develop a Null and Alternative Hypothesis.

The " = " goes with **Ho.** We test **Ha.**

The Hypothesis will be   **Ho:** $\mu1 = \mu2 = \mu3 = \ldots = \mu n$ (All means are equal)

Ha: at least one mean is different from the others.

The Test Statistic **F** = the variance between samples / the variance within samples.

= **MS treatment / MS error**.

(sample is also called treatment or factor)

To look up the **F critical value** we need: the numerator degrees of freedom (**k-1**)

the denominator degrees of freedom **k(n-1)**

Where **"k"** is the number of different samples (*also called treatments, or factors*)

"n" is the number of items within each sample.

In a **One Way ANOVA** we are comparing only **one** variable from each sample.

Enter each sample into its own LIST.(sample1 into LIST1, sample2 into LIST2, sample3 into LIST3, etc.)

Since the TI-83PLUS gives a p-value we will **reject Ho if p < alpha.**

The calculator also gives the **F** Statistic, Sum of Squares(**SS**), Mean Squares(**MS**), and the pooled deviation(**Sxp**)..

Example 1 (One Way ANOVA)

Hot peppers are officially measured in laboratory units called scovill units. On a common scale they are "taste tested" and ranked on a scale from 1 to 10 with 1 the mildest, 10 hottest. Four different peppers were considered for the "Salsa in a jar" from section #7. The taste test rankings from 12 of each type of pepper were as follows:

Jalapenos	Tai Red	Serrano	Scotch Bonnet
7.4	8.9	8.6	8.8
6.0	9.0	8.6	8.6
7.4	6.0	6.2	8.5
4.2	6.0	10.0	8.9
7.4	6.5	6.2	8.3
5.2	8.2	9.5	8.5
6.5	8.4	7.9	9.1
6.8	5.4	6.2	6.8
6.2	8.5	9.4	9.1
6.6	7.9	7.7	5.6
6.2	5.7	8.6	8.9
6.0	8.8	8.5	9.4

Develop the Null and Alternative Hypothesis, and using $\alpha = 0.05$ test your hypothesis. State your conclusion. Find:
a) the variance between the different types of peppers,
b) variance within each type of pepper,
c) the F Test Statistic,
d) the F critical value. Develop the Null and Alternative Hypothesis, and using $\alpha = 0.05$ test your hypothesis.

We will begin by entering the data into the appropriate LISTS.
Press STAT.

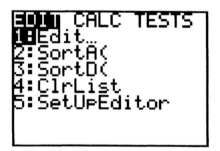

Press **ENTER** (this screen will appear) *[always start from a clear list]*

L1	L2	L3	1
▮▮▮▮	------	------	

L1(1) =

Next enter each piece of data from sample1 into LIST1, sample2 into LIST2, etc.

(When you've finished all four LIST you should be looking at this screen)

L2	L3	L4	4
8.4	7.9	9.1	
5.4	6.2	6.8	
8.5	9.4	9.1	
7.9	7.7	5.6	
5.7	8.6	8.9	
8.8	8.5	9.4	
------	------	▮▮▮▮	

L4(13) =

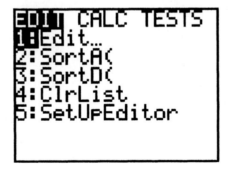

```
EDIT CALC TESTS
1:Edit…
2:SortA(
3:SortD(
4:ClrList
5:SetUpEditor
```

Now *press* **STAT**

Arrow right to **"TESTS"** and **Arrow up** to "**F : ANOVA (** "

```
EDIT CALC TESTS
0↑2-SampTInt…
A:1-PropZInt…
B:2-PropZInt…
C:χ²-Test…
D:2-SampFTest…
E:LinRegTTest…
F:ANOVA(
```

Press ENTER (this screen appears)

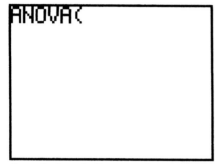

Here we **must** enter **all factors** we want to test.
For our problem it will be **L1, L2, L3, L4** .

so *press*

(see below left screen)

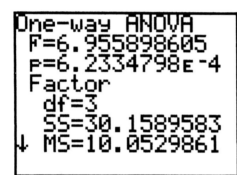

This screen can be seen by pressing the **Arrow down** *key* ———\

As you can see from the screen the **MS Factor = 10.05**
(*this is the amount of variation between pepper types*).
If we Arrow down we see that the **MS Error = 1.44**
(*this is the amount of variance within each type of pepper*).
The **F Test Statistic** is seen to be = **6.96.**
The Null Hypothesis is   Ho: $\mu 1 = \mu 2 = \mu 3 = \mu 4$
The Alternative Hypothesis is   Ha : at least one mean is different.

The p-value = 0.00062 < 0.05   Therefore we should **reject Ho.**

From the tables in the Textbook we see that the **F c.v. = 2.83** [*k=3, n(k-1)=44*]
Since our **F Statistic = 6.96 > 2.83.** We would reject Ho.

In conclusion we say that at the 0.05 level of significance there is sufficient evidence to reject the claim that all four pepper types have the same mean "taste test" ranking.

Example 2

Suppose there are three companies each offering a different additive to be tested for a new fuel supplement that should increase horsepower. Each company claims that their additive is "just as effective as the other" treatments for increasing horsepower. Construct an ANOVA table from the data below.
Is there evidence of differences between the mean horsepower increases of the three different additives at $\alpha = 0.05$? At $\alpha = 0.10$? At what level of significance does there appear to be a difference?

Additive 1	Additive 2	Additive 3
3.0	5.4	1.3
1.4	2.0	0.7
4.1	4.8	2.2
5.5	3.8	
2.3	3.5	

L1	L2	L3	3
3.9	5.4	1.3	
1.4	2	.7	
4.1	4.8	2.2	
5.5	3.8		
2.3	3.5		
------	------		

L3(4) =

We begin by entering all data into the appropriate list.

Note: In ANOVA it is not necessary that the list be of equal length.

```
EDIT CALC TESTS
0↑2-SampTInt...
A:1-PropZInt...
B:2-PropZInt...
C:X²-Test...
D:2-SampFTest...
E:LinRegTTest...
F:ANOVA(
```

Press: STAT

Arrow Left to "TESTS" and **Arrow up** to "F : ANOVA("

```
ANOVA(L1,L2,L3)■
```

Press: ENTER

For ANOVA you simply enter each list where you have the data.

For this problem I will enter L1, L2, L3 as I used said lists.

Press:

Press: ENTER   To see all the results you must arrow down.

```
One-way ANOVA          One-way ANOVA
 F=3.387603014         ↑ MS=6.21015385
 p=.0752767198          Error
 Factor                  df=10
  df=2                   SS=18.332
  SS=12.4203077          MS=1.8332
↓ MS=6.21015385         Sxp=1.35395716
■                      ■
```

All values requested can be read directly from the screens as the calculator uses standard notation. Recall our hypothesis for ANOVA

Ho: all means are equal

H1: at least one mean is different

We see from the first screen the p-value is **.075** which is not less than   .05 therefore we **do not reject Ho** at $\alpha = 0.05$.

We also see from this screen 0.075 is less than 0.10 therefore **we do reject Ho** at $\alpha = 0.10$.

Since the p-value = 0.75 that is the significance level at which we would indicate there is a difference between at least two of the means.

χ2 Test
Finding p-values for Contingency Tables on the TI-83

This test is also called the "Test for Independence". The TI-83PLUS has a built-in χ2 function, found under the "distr" menu. Recall the basis for the chi-squared test; two events are independent if $P(A \cap B) = P(A) * P(B)$.
As always the calculator returns the p-value and we reject Ho if $p < \alpha$.
The Hypotheses are

     Ho : The matrix entries represents independent events.

     Ha : The matrix entries represent events which are not independent.

All we need to do is enter the **observed** values as Matrix**[A],** and the **expected** values as Matrix **[B].** *To calculate each entry for the expected Matrix, [B] simply multiply that row total and that column total then divide the product by the grand total.*

Example : A study of 500 males by a graduate statistics student was conducted to determine whether religious affiliation had an effect on divorce rate. At the 99% level of confidence test to see whether there is sufficient evidence to conclude religious affiliation does have an effect on divorce rate. The collected data is as follows:

	Religious affiliation					Totals
	A	B	C	D	O	
Divorced	39	19	12	28	18	116
Not Divorced	172	61	44	70	37	384
Totals	211	80	56	98	55	500

Grand Total

Our **Observed** Matrix will be **[A]** =

$$\begin{vmatrix} 39 & 19 & 12 & 28 & 18 \\ 172 & 61 & 44 & 70 & 37 \end{vmatrix}$$

Our **Expected** Matrix will be **[B]** =

$$\begin{vmatrix} 48.952 & 18.56 & 12.992 & 22.736 & 12.76 \\ 162.05 & 61.44 & 43.008 & 75.264 & 42.24 \end{vmatrix}$$

The hypothesis for this problem is as follows:

     Ho: The Matrix entries represent Independent events.

     Ha: The Matrix entries represent events that **are not** independent.

First, access the Matrix Menu and enter all values for both Matrices.

Press **MATRIX** **Arrow right** to "**EDIT**".   "**1 : [A] 1x1**" will be highlighted,
Press **ENTER**   Enter the dimensions of our Observed Matrix. (2 by 5)
(see screen below right)

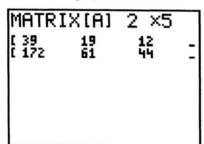

Enter all values (see screen above right)   Next we must edit Matrix [B].
      Press **MATRIX**   **Arrow Right to** "**EDIT**".
  " **1 : [A] 1x1** " will be highlighted.
Press **ENTER** Enter the dimensions of our Expected Matrix.
(*same as above*) Enter all expected values* (see screen below)

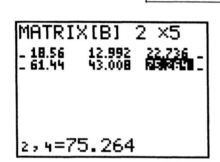

> * Each expected value entry is
> the product of (that row total) *
> (that column total) / grand total.

Next Perform the $\chi2$ – **Test**. *Press* **STAT** Arrow right to " **TESTS** "
      Arrow up to "**C : $\chi2$ – Test…**" (see screen below left)

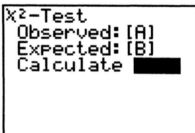

Press **ENTER** (see screen above right) Match these settings. Observed: **[A]**

Expected: **[B]. Arrow down** to "**Calculate**"

Press ENTER (see screen below)

```
X²-Test
  X²=7.135464193
  P=.128900399
  df=4

█
```

 As you can see from the screen the **p-value = 0.129**.
Since the p-value is **not less** than α we **do not** reject Ho.
There is not statistical evidence at the $\alpha = 0.01$ level to conclude the male
divorce rate depends on religious affiliation.

Example 2

Test the Null Hypothesis of Independence of the two classifications A & B
using the contingency table given. Use $\alpha = 0.05$

	B1	B2	B3
A1	40	72	42
A2	63	53	70
A3	31	38	30

To perform the χ^2 test we first enter the observed data into Matrix A and the
expected data into Matrix B. From there we perform the χ^2 test using
$\alpha = .05$ Press: 2nd x⁻¹

```
NAMES MATH EDIT
1:[A]
2:[B]
3:[C]
4:[D]
5:[E]
6:[F]
7↓[G]
```

Arrow Right to **EDIT** and
Press: ENTER

Enter the dimensions of your matrix.
For this problem it is a 3 X 3

Enter each value pressing ENTER after each piece of data.

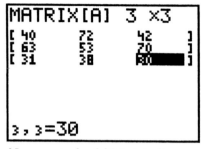

After you have completed Matrix A
you must enter the expected values for Matrix
B.

Now on to build Matrix B.

Press: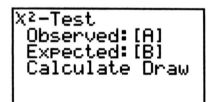

Arrow Right to **EDIT** then **Arrow Down** and highlight **2:[B]** then
Press: ENTER

Recall: your Expected Matrix must be the same Dimension as your Observed
Matrix.

Enter all values pressing ENTER after each piece of data.

After you have entered all the data into the matrices *press:* STAT
Arrow Left to **TESTS** and **Arrow Up** to **C: χ^2 –Test….**
Press: ENTER

```
X²-Test
  Observed: [A]
  Expected: [B]
  Calculate Draw
```

This is the Chi square test. Recall we placed
the Observed values into Matrix A and the
Expected values into Matrix B.

Now, **Arrow Down** to **Calculate** and
Press: ENTER

```
X²-Test
 X²=12.32703245
 P=.0150780495
 df=4

■
```

As can be seen from the screen the χ^2 value
is **12.327**

*The associated p-value is **.015**; which is not less than **.01** therefore we cannot reject Ho: the events are Independent.*

We therefore conclude that **A** and **B** are **Independent events**. ☺

Normal Probability Plots

Use this data set to graph a Normal Probability plot.

5.9	5.3	1.6	7.4	8.6	1.2	2.1
4.0	7.3	8.4	8.9	6.7	4.5	6.3
7.6	9.7	3.5	1.1	4.3	3.3	8.4
1.6	8.2	6.5	1.1	5.0	9.4	6.4

First enter the data into the calculator. I will use list 1.

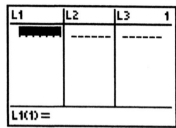

Press: STAT ENTER

This will take you to the Lists Menu.

Clear any old data from the list as it may interfere with this new problem.

After you have entered all the data
Press: 2nd Y=

"1:Plot1..." *should be highlighted.*

Press: ENTER

Make sure **"On"** *is highlighted*

Press: ENTER
(Note: the switch is moved to **"On"***)*

Arrow down and right to highlight the last Plot option.

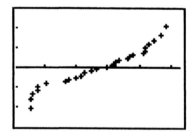

For **Data List** *I entered* **L1** *as that is where I placed my data.*

For **Data Axis** *highlight* **X** *and*
press: ENTER
Next *Press:* ZOOM 9

As you can see from the screen there is a noticeable curve.
(perhaps a cubic model would be appropriate here or a cube root transformation of the data)

It does not appear Normally Distributed.

Two Sample F-Test

Perform an F-Test on the calculator using the following data sets:
Sample 1:   3.1   4.3   1.2   1.7   0.6   3.4
Sample 2:   2.3   1.4   3.7   8.9

> No matter what order the text puts the data in, on the calculator the data set that has the **largest variance is called sample 1 !**
> This only applies to F-Test done on the calculator.

The Hypothesis for the F-Test are
$$H_o: \sigma_1 = \sigma_2$$
$$H_a: \sigma_1 \neq \sigma_2 \text{, and we will reject Ho if our p-value} < \alpha.$$

Press: STAT

```
EDIT CALC TESTS
0↑2-SampTInt...
A:1-PropZInt...
B:2-PropZInt...
C:X²-Test...
D:2-SampFTest...
E:LinRegTTest...
F:ANOVA(
```

Arrow Left to **TESTS** and **Arrow up** to
D: 2-SampFTest...

Press: ENTER

Once again we choose Data as we will enter the statistics ourselves.

```
2-SampFTest
  Inpt:DATA Stats
  List1:L₂
  List2:L₁ ◄
  Freq1:1
  Freq2:1
  σ1:≠σ2 <σ2 >σ2 ◄
  Calculate Draw
```

Note the order: the calculator always puts List 2 on top(it must be the sample with the largest variance)
The test line still must match Ha.

```
2-SampFTest
  σ1≠σ2
  F=4.237545365
  p=.0071180665
  Sx1=.202132858
  Sx2=.098192821
↓x̄1=4.199230769
■
```

After you adjust all fields for your problem
Arrow Down to **Calculate** and *Press:* ENTER

As can be seen from the screen the p-value is .007 which is less than .10 therefore we **reject Ho**.

At the $\alpha = .10$ level the two variances are not equal.

ERROR Messages

DIM MISMATCH is by far the most common **Error** message.

```
ERR:DIM MISMATCH
1∎Quit
```

To clear this message
press CLEAR several times

and/or

2nd MODE then CLEAR

The steps above will return you to the home screen, but they will not remedy the reason for the error! This message is displayed indicating an error in one of two main categories:

A   the Lists are different lengths (dimensions)
B   the designated List may be empty

Error Category A. for DIM MISMATCH

Look at this screen below carefully.

```
L1      L2      L3      2

40      38      2
80      85      -5
25      19      6
50      52      -2
58      58      0
------  51      ------

L2(11) =
```

The error at the top of this page was given when I tried ZOOM ▓ *using* **List1 , List 2** to graph a Histogram.

Look carefully at List 1 and List 2.
They are different lengths.

I thought I was careful in entering the data, yet I received the ERROR message.

```
Plot1 Plot2 Plot3
  ∎Off
Type: ⌐ ⌐ ⊥
      ⊞ ⊞ ∠
Xlist:L1
Freq:L2
```

First I went back to the Stat Plot.

After checking my Stat Plot and seeing that everything looked correct I decided to check the actual data.

That is when I found the error!   Lists must be the same length!

Error Category B for DIM MISMATCH

I was trying to graph a Box & Whisker plot when I received this message:

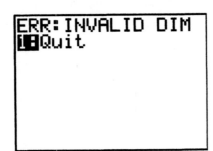

I went to **Stat Plot** and looked at the set-up. Everything seemed to be correct.

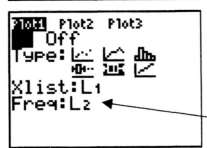

I went to the **Lists** to make sure the Lists were the same length.

They looked the same length.

BUT look closely at the very top of the screen. **L1** **L3** ???

L1	L3	L4	2
70	40		
40	21		
80	70		
25	45		
50	65		
58	65		

L3(10) =

Where is **L2** ?
That is where I told the calculator to find the Frequencies.

I had mistakenly deleted List 2 when I was trying to clear it for this problem.

Apparently, I pressed **DEL** instead of **CLEAR** and I deleted List 2!

At this point I could just go to Stat Plot and replace **L2** with **L3** and I will get my Box & Whisker plot, but that will not return my List 2.

To return any or all the lists to the editor follow these steps:

From the home screen *Press:* STAT
Arrow down to **"5:SetUpEditor"**

Press: ENTER ENTER

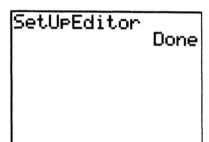

This screen tells me that I have corrected my deletion and that all Lists are back to where they should be ☺

To verify I *Press:* STAT ENTER
I see that List 2 is back between List 1 and List 3 where it belongs.

L1	L2	L3	1
30	------	25	
20		32	
60		34	
70		40	
40		21	
80		70	
25		45	

L1(1)=30

Now, to get the Box & Whisker plot I simply go back to Stat Plot and change the frequency list from **L2** to **L3**.

Or
Enter the frequencies into List 2.

You can clear the error message by following the same steps as above.

INVALID DIM is another ERROR message that you may see:

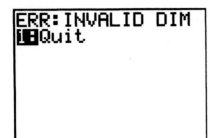

This error occurs when there is an entry that doesn't "make sense" to the calculator. It most often occurs when you mistakenly enter a stray keystroke.

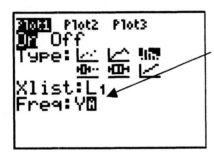

I was trying to graph a Histogram when I mistakenly entered this **"Y"** when I thought I was entering a **"1"** for **Freq:**
To enter a **"1"** you must
Press: ALPHA 1

When you arrow down to **Xlist:** & **Freq:** *the calculator is already in* **ALPHA MODE** *so by pressing* ALPHA *you return the calculator to* **STANDARD MODE**.
Yes, I know it seems backwards but it works☺

You can clear the error message by following the same steps as above.

SYNTAX is another **ERROR** message that occurs with some regularity.

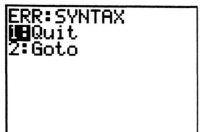

This error occurs when the calculator is expecting a particular type or number of response and you have neglected to give it what it wants.

This particular screen appeared when I entered a "-" sign instead of a "(-)" sign when I was adjusting the window.

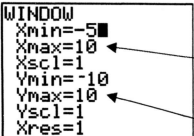

Please note the position and size of the subtraction sign.

It is smaller and placed higher than the negative sign.

When I pressed ENTER I received the above error message.
You must also be careful when using **any** of the functions from the **Distributions Menu.**

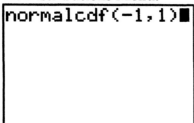

Here I am trying to find the area under the standard normal distribution curve between **negative 1 and positive 1** , but what I've entered is **subtract 1 comma 1.**

Subtract 1 comma 1 makes no sense and the calculator returns the following error message:

You must take care to use the correct syntax when entering values into your calculator ☺

You can clear this error message following the same steps as above.

DOMAIN is yet another **error** message that can occur.

This error occurs when you have entered a value that is outside the expected *domain* (remember algebra)

You can clear this error message following the same steps as above.

I was trying to perform a 1-Proportion Z-Test when I received the error message above.

The error occurred at the very first line.
I entered the whole number "30" for the p_0 :

The calculator is expecting a decimal (number between 0 and 1)
Even though I meant 30% the correct entry would be " .30 "
This error can occur when you are using any of the Statistical TESTS or Distributions.

```
ERR:DOMAIN
1:Quit
2:Goto
```

Here is another example of a value outside the expected domain that resulted in this error message.

I was trying to calculate the probability for a problem using the binomial distribution function.

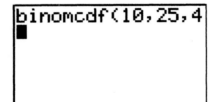

As you can see the second entry is " 25 "
It is the percent that was listed in my book, but recall the proper notation for 25% is " .25 " ; a decimal.

I should have entered " .25 " instead of " 25 "

Programs

Program 1

Baye's Formula : Calculates the conditional probability of event A given the probability of event B. You need to enter: the probability of A , the probability of $(B \mid A)$, the probability of $(B \mid A^c)$

Disp "THIS"
Disp "PROGRAM"
Disp "WILL CALCULATE"
Disp "THE PROBABILITY"
Disp "OF (A $\mid$ B)"
Disp "ENTER EACH OF"
Disp "THE FOLLOWING"
Input "P(A)=",A
Input "P(B $\mid$ A)=",C
Input "P(B $\mid$ A^c)=",D
C*A/((C*A)+D*(1-A))$\rightarrow$E
Disp " P(A $\mid$ B)=",E
Stop

Program 2

Bernoulli : This is a distribution function which will give the probability of a success, the probability of a failure , the mean, and the standard deviation for a Bernoulli Distribution. You need to enter: the probability of a success.

Disp "PLEASE ENTER"
Disp "THE PROBABILITY"
Disp "OF SUCCESS 'P'"
Input "p=",A
(A^0)(1-A)^(1-0)$\rightarrow$B
(A^1)(1-A)^(1-1)$\rightarrow$C
A*(1-A)$\rightarrow$D
Disp "THE MEAN IS",A$\blacktriangleright$Frac
Pause
Disp "THE VAR IS",D$\blacktriangleright$Frac
Pause
Disp " "
Disp " "
Disp "THE PROBABILITY"
Disp "OF NO SUCCESS"
Disp "P(X=0)",B$\blacktriangleright$Frac
Pause

Disp " "
Disp " "
Disp "THE PROBABILITY"
Disp "OF 1 SUCCESS"
Disp "P(X=1)IS",C$\blacktriangleright$Frac
STOP

Program 3
Exponential : This program gives the area under the exponential curve
between two bounds and will draw the graph of that Exponential Distribution.
It shows the lower, upper bounds along with the probability that x is between
those bounds. You need to enter: μ , lower bound , upper bound.
Disp "EXPONENTIAL"
Disp "DISTRIBUTION"
Disp " THIS PROGRAM"
Disp "WILL GIVE AREA"
Disp "BETWEEN LOWER,"
Disp "UPPER BOUNDS"
Input "MU=",U
Disp "LOWER BOUND="
Input A
Disp "UPPER BOUND="
Input B
0→Xmin
(8*U)→Xmax
0→Ymin
(1/U)→Ymax
U→Xscl
ClrDraw
PlotsOff
FnOff
ClrAllLists
seq((1/U)ë^(úX/U),X,A,B,1)→L2,
seq(J,J,A,B,1)→L1
ExpReg L1,L2,Y1
fnInt(Y1,X,A,B,.5)→T
Disp ""
Disp ""
Disp "AREA IS",T   ⟶   Shade(0,Y1,A,B)
Disp ""   End
Disp "ENTER 1 TO"   Disp ""
Disp "SEE DISPLAY"   Disp ""
Disp ""   Disp ""
Input "0 TO END",H   Disp ""
If H=1   Disp "AREA IS",T
Then ─────────────────────────   Stop

Program 4
Hypergeometric cdf : This program will calculate the cumulative probability of an event that follows a hypergeometric distribution. It gives the cumulative probability of 0 successes, 1 success, …. up to whatever value you enter as x. **N** is the total number of items, **n** is the number of items sampled, '**type-1**' is the number of defective items from the population, **X** is the maximum number of desired defective items in the sample. You must enter: N, n, Type-1, x

```
Disp "ENTER"
Disp " TOTAL NUMBER"
Disp "OF ITEMS"
Input "N=",N
Disp "ENTER"
Disp " NUMBER OF"
Disp "TYPE-1 ITEMS"
Input "M=",M
Disp "ENTER"
Disp " NUMBER OF"
Disp "REMOVED ITEMS"
Input "n=",A
Disp "ENTER  LARGEST"
Disp "NUMBER  DESIRED"
Disp " TYPE-1  ITEMS"
Input "X=",X
0→Z
For(Y,0,X)
(M nCr Y)→V
(N-M) nCr (A-Y)→W
(V*W)/(N nCr A)→S
(Z+S)→Z
Disp "THE PROBABILITY"
Disp " DRAWING ≤",Y
Disp " TYPE-1  ITEMS"
Disp "FROM THIS GROUP"
Disp "IS",Z▶Frac
Pause
End
Stop
```

Program 5
Hypergeometric pdf: This program gives the probability of exactly X
successes of a random variable that follows a Hypergeometric Distribution.
N is the total number of items, **n** is the number of items sampled, '**type-1**' is
the number of defective items from the population, **X** is the number of desired
defective items in the sample. You must enter: N, n, Type-1, X

```
Disp "ENTER"
Disp "THE TOTAL NUMBER"
Disp "OF ITEMS"
Input "N=",N
Disp "ENTER"
Disp "THE NUMBER OF"
Disp "TYPE-1 ITEMS"
Input "M=",M
Disp "ENTER"
Disp "THE NUMBER OF"
Disp "REMOVED ITEMS"
Input "n=",A
Disp "ENTER NUMBER"
Disp "OF DESIRED"
Disp "TYPE-1 ITEMS"
Input "X=",X
(M nCr X)→V
(N-M) nCr (A-X)→W
(V*W)/(N nCr A)→Z
Disp "THE PROBABILITY"
Disp "OF EXACTLY X"
Disp "TYPE-1 ITEMS"
Disp "FROM THIS GROUP"
Disp " P(X=X) IS",Z▶Frac
STOP
Stop
```